High-Leade...
High-Impact Schools:
The Actions
That Matter Most

Pamela S. Salazar

Routledge
Taylor & Francis Group

LONDON AND NEW YORK

First published 2008 by Eye on Education

Published 2013 by Routledge

2 Park Square, Milton Park, Abingdon, Oxfordshire OX14 4RN

Simultaneously published in the USA and Canada by Routledge

711 Third Avenue, New York, NY 10017

Routledge is an imprint of the Taylor & Francis Group, an informa business

Copyright © 2008 Taylor & Francis

Salazar, Pam.
  High-impact leadership for high-impact schools : the actions that matter most / Pam Salazar.
    p. cm.
  ISBN-13: 978-1-59667-076-1
  1. Educational leadership—United States. 2. Educational accountability—United States. 3. Academic achievement—United States. I. Title.
  LB2805.S2637 2008
  371.2—dc22

                                          2007049452

Dedication

To my parents, Ray and JoAnn Cummins who have always been so proud of me and have helped me achieve whatever success I have had. Thank you Mom and Dad for all of your love and encouragement and belief in me.

To my husband, Tom, without whose love, collaboration, and support, this book would never have been possible. You are my best friend, my inspiration, and the most patient man alive to listen to every single word in this book as I tried to put my thoughts to paper.

To my children, Jason, Cortney, and Cresen, how proud I am of you—you are the never-ending joy in our lives. Thank you for continually telling me that I could do this.

To my grandchildren, Jason Jr., Ryan, and Jenna, you are talented in so many ways, and we look forward to watching you grow.

To my brother, Ray, you have always been there for me, encouraging me and challenging me to think about the hard problems, the difficult decisions, and the necessary actions that must be taken to make an impact. I am blessed to have such insightful and thought-provoking conversations with someone I love and admire so much. And this is amazing when I remember what a pain in the rear you were when you were a student in my physics class. Word to the wise … tough to be your brother's teacher in high school.

To my very dear friend, Carol Ryan, who has supported me over some 30 years as both a friend and a colleague. Thank you, thank you, for your untiring assistance, patience, and infinite wisdom for helping me turn my words into organized writing.

To my very dear friend, Carol Ross, who from the first day I started teaching, mentored me and planted the seed for this book, though little did we know it at the time. You have been an extraordinary friend, with more influence in my life than you will ever know.

To my friends and colleagues who continually give so much of themselves each and every day to ensure that our students have a bright future. Their dedication and courageous work is so frequently overlooked; yet, it is their work that has given me the opportunity to write about how passionate and committed educators can truly reshape the lives of children. My heartfelt thanks goes out to each of your for your loyalty to education.

To my publisher, Robert Sickles, who motivated me to write this book and without his support, this book would not have evolved. Thank you, Bob, for your brilliant advice and never-wavering encouragement.

Table of Contents

Foreword

As a practicing or aspiring school leader, researcher, or academician, you have hundreds of choices from the menu of virtual and print books about how to lead schools. Which of this plethora of "how-to-guides" offers the greatest potential for influencing the practice of school leadership and subsequently creating schools that make a difference?

High-Impact Leadership for High-Impact Schools: The Actions That Matter Most is a must read for all practicing and aspiring school leaders. Pam Salazar has skillfully blended her experiences as a teacher, assistant principal, principal, principal developer, and academician to create this practitioner friendly resource. Global positioning systems (GPS) guide today's travel informing us about the shortest, most scenic, or recommended route to our destination. Consider this book your GPS for leading schools on a journey to excellence. The content won't guide you along the most scenic, the least bumpy, or the shortest path to your destination but it will instruct you along the most effective route to your target of creating a high performing school.

The substance of this book provides a logical path of leadership actions that make a difference. Rooted in solid theory, substantiated by recent research, and written for practical application, the five steps for action provide a detailed rationale, action plan, and tools for focusing everyone's attention on teaching and learning. These actions will ensure a rigorous standard of student performance and will build a work culture that promotes collaboration, knowledge sharing, and collective responsibility for improving teaching and learning. This book will help you align resources, structures, time, and decisions with a focused improvement agenda.

Just as travel to unfamiliar destinations is precisely aided by electronic navigation, *High-Impact Leadership for High-Impact Schools: The Actions That Matter Most* can chart the leadership actions necessary for creating high performing schools that make a difference.

Richard A. Flanary
NASSP
Director of Professional Development Services

About the Author

Pamela S. Salazar spent 30 years in public school education where she served as a middle school and high school teacher, department chair, assistant principal, principal, and principal on special assignment for mentoring and coaching new principals. She recently entered higher education, where she is an assistant professor and coordinator of the collaborative principal preparation program in the Department of Educational Leadership at the University of Nevada, Las Vegas teaching courses in instructional leadership, school improvement, professional development, and leading change. Her research areas include leadership, the principalship, and professional development.

Pam has written numerous articles, chapters, and monographs in the areas of instructional leadership, professional development, and the principalship. She has made over 100 presentations, including district, state, regional, and national conferences, for both administrators and teachers on becoming more effective at creating high-performing schools. She is the coeditor of *The Rural Educator,* an international journal. Her editorial board service has included: *NASSP Bulletin, NASSP Connections, Connexions, Journal of Women in Educational Leadership, Education Leadership Review,* and the *Journal of School Public Relations.*

Pam is married to Tom, and they have three children, Jason, Cortney, and Cresen, plus three grandchildren, Jason Jr., Ryan, and Jenna.

Introduction

Framework for Understanding High-Impact Schools— Five Areas for Action

The educational challenge of the twenty-first century is to achieve high levels of learning for each and every student. As increased accountability becomes the norm, leadership becomes more challenging and demanding. In today's complex world, in schools beset with new kinds of issues and problems, the ability of the principal to improve the effectiveness of the school becomes the critical element in determining the kind of impact that the school will have on its students.

High-impact schools are typically led by highly effective principals—principals whose leadership positively impacts the school's success. And schools that achieve higher than expected results and achieve them faster are led by higher-impact principals than schools that do not achieve high results. There is an abundance of research that concludes that school leadership has a significant effect on student learning. In fact, nearly 25% of the in-school factors affecting student achievement can be attributed directly to the quality and effectiveness of the principal. This is second only to the effects of teacher instruction, which is shaped by the way principals select, support, and develop their teachers. And, since principals select, train, manage, support, develop, evaluate, and create the culture for teachers, the quality of teachers is greatly dependent on the effectiveness of the principal. The bottom line is that the quality and effectiveness of school principals determine the impact that schools have on students.

We have learned much about high performing schools over the past ten years. Some schools do succeed at helping all their students achieve, regardless of their background or socioeconomic conditions. The challenge is to determine how high-achieving schools break the usual pattern of low achievement. And the bigger question is what lessons can we learn from these schools that can be transferred to other schools that are struggling to meet the needs of every student? In particular, what leadership behaviors and decisions are different in high-impact schools than in average-impact schools?

Although public schools are responsible for educating all students, they historically have had greater success educating middle-to-upper income and white students than they have had with poor and minority students. Nearly all the worst-performing schools across the country are high-poverty schools. But there are also striking exceptions to the low income/low performance pattern. There are enough schools that defy the trend to prove that the background of the student body does not have to determine achievement results.

So, what practices make the difference? What separates high-impact schools from average-impact schools? What seems to contribute to high student performance? There are no shortcuts to school success, but a serious examination of leadership practices that can drive the quality and effectiveness of our schools appears to be the most significant way we can offer our neediest students better support to help them reach high standards of excellence. Effective educational success depends on high-impact leadership.

High-impact leadership means creating powerful, equitable learning opportunities for both students and teachers and motivating individuals to take advantage of those opportunities. Making an impact means taking action. How do we implement the needed reforms in a deliberate high-quality way? How can we take powerful ideas and implement them to meet the urgent educational needs of children as quickly as possible? This book is about just that—taking actions that have a high impact on student outcomes, which, in turn have a high impact on school success. High-impact leaders can accomplish these outcomes by focusing on five areas for action that together make it more likely that every student will have access to a high-quality and equitable learning opportunity.

Five Areas for Action

1. *It's about the mission not the mission statement.* It all starts with beliefs and values—principals cannot expect results if there is not a whole-school commitment to every student's success. Principals must focus everyone's attention persistently and relentlessly on learning and teaching.

2. *High expectations for each and every student.* In high-impact schools, teachers engage students in a learning process that maximizes excellence and equity. Because teachers make no assumptions about why students cannot learn, no self-fulfilling prophecies prevail. Principals must focus on a learning agenda that ensures a rigorous standard of student performance and provides the needed supports for students to succeed.

3. *Building communities of learners.* Strong, learning-focused communities offer professional support and provide learning opportunities and mutual accountability for improving instruction. Principals must build a work culture that promotes collaboration, knowledge sharing, and collective responsibility for improving teaching and learning.

4. *Teachers are the silver bullet.* Competent, caring, and qualified teachers must be in every classroom. Individual teachers have a profound influence on student learning, and the strategies they use to guide classroom practice should maximize the possibility of enhancing student achievement. Principals must help teachers succeed through supervision practices and reflective dialogue.

5. *Creating a coherent system for continuous improvement.* Organizational processes and practices are critical to the development of a coherent system of support for the improvement of teaching and learning. School effectiveness and the level of impact on student learning are dependent on the alignment of resources, structures, time, and decisions with each other and with a focused improvement agenda.

In the following chapters, we will expand on these key ideas. We will look at specific knowledge and practical strategies that point leaders toward promising possibilities of becoming high-impact leaders. The overall framework offers perspectives, tools, and tactics to make student learning more powerful and equitable with the focus on becoming a high-impact school.

Chapter 1

It's About the Mission, Not the Mission Statement

The soul never thinks without a picture.

—Aristotle

It all starts with beliefs, values, and purpose—principals cannot expect results if there is not a whole-school commitment to every student's success. Principals must focus everyone's attention persistently and relentlessly on learning and teaching.

When you walk into a school that has a purpose and a vision, you can feel it. When you talk with the teachers in such a school, they will tell you they are excited about what they are doing. They believe in what they are doing. They believe they make a difference in their students' lives each and every day. They are on a mission.

High-Impact Leaders Ask:

- ◆ What is our fundamental reason for existence? What do we aspire to achieve and to become? What business are we in?
- ◆ Does the school have a shared vision and core values? Is there a mission that unites all? Is there a deep understanding of the mission by all?
- ◆ Are there common practices and beliefs that effectively express the values and mission? Are the needs of all met?
- ◆ What's the picture of our culture and school if they are to be highly successful? What should be important for our school?
- ◆ Does the school have a concrete, shared, well-defined action plan that effectively expresses the vision, mission, and shared beliefs?

Creating and Illuminating a Vision

Creating a shared vision for your school is key to creating a high-impact school. High-impact leaders articulate a unifying vision that ties the faculty, staff, students, and parent community together. The vision of the school serves as a coherent picture of how the school will function when the core beliefs are practiced.

Groups of people aligned behind shared vision, values, and teaching beliefs provide the cornerstone for school success. Inspiring, energizing, and motivating stakeholders around the vision create momentum for development and improvement. High-impact leaders are able to articulate their philosophies and visions to members of the school community. These leaders are able to persuade and lead others to support a vision of education that becomes the driving force for the school. They are a dynamic force that develops that understanding in others and enlists them to support that vision.

High-impact leaders passionately believe they can make a difference. They translate the vision from words to pictures with a vivid description of what life will be like when the school's goal is achieved. They create an ideal and unique image of what the school could become. Through their magnetism and quiet persuasion (or sometimes not so quiet), they enlist others in their dreams. They breathe life into their vision and get people to see the exciting possibilities. They look for innovative approaches and encourage risk taking. They foster collaboration and spirited teamwork. They understand that mutual respect and an atmosphere of trust and personal dignity sustain extraordinary efforts. High-impact leaders are able to help others see themselves present in the shared vision.

High-impact leaders believe that dreams can become reality. They believe in vision, trust, teamwork, and the power of relationships. They see their role defined by the need to create the conditions for new ideas to flourish. They stand firm against forces of the status quo, and they give all involved the courage to continue the quest. Their leadership propels the school forward.

High-impact leaders embody a style of influence that attracts and energizes people to enlist in an exciting vision of the future. These leaders form a powerful guiding coalition to drive the vision. They find the right people, people with strong position power, broad expertise, and high credibility. They articulate and embody the ideals of the school and they build a team vision to take care of all kids and to increase learner outcomes. Such inspired and informed leadership leads to the success of the school.

Leaders like these are visionaries. They create transforming visions of schools. There is a big difference between being a school with a vision statement and becoming a truly visionary school.

Leaders of high-impact schools have the ability to convert their dreams for the future into viable activities in which their followers are willing to believe and work. High-impact leaders empower others to act on the vision.

Such leaders develop a vision that is comprehensive and detailed. People must know the how, why, what, and when of the dream. The vision must be positive and inspiring—it must be worth the efforts of all those onboard. When a school lives its vision and aligns its work with that vision, a visitor can sense what that vision is without ever reading it on a plaque or banner.

These leaders reflect and think about their own vision. They are able to expand their personal visions into a shared vision that elicits commitment. By their certainty of what the learning community should be, they bring a sense of purpose to all.

The high-impact leader possesses a clear, vivid mental picture or image of the ideal school. Such leaders help other people in the school community move toward that mental image and, when necessary, they have the courage to say "No" to things that don't fit the vision and "Yes" to things that do. For example, if a new program is presented to the school as part of a new initiative, but the program doesn't fit or align with the direction of the school, then the program is declined. Data is used to support the reason for saying no and to demonstrate how this new program does not facilitate the envisioned future. These leaders know where the school is headed and what outcomes are sought, and they do not get caught up in installing new programs just because they are there. High-impact leaders are active advocates of the school's vision.

The first step in developing a more effective school is describing what you seek to become. High-impact leaders articulate a clear vision for the school and its efforts. They identify where they want to go in relation to where they are now based on school data. In high-impact schools, the vision is imaginable and conveys a picture of what the future will be. It is desirable and appeals to the long-term interests of the teachers and the students. It is feasible and comprises realistic, attainable goals. It is focused—clear enough to provide guidance in decision making, but also flexible enough to allow individual initiative and different actions caused by changing conditions. The vision is easy to communicate; it can be easily explained.

It is important to make the distinction between a vision statement and the vision itself. The writing and posting of vision statements is a common practice in schools. Unfortunately, this activity does not lead to the genuine visioning that needs to take place. Words on a paper do not translate to the dynamic power of the vision of the school. While the mission or vision statement may serve an important purpose, the real promise of a vision statement is the power that it has to drive the school forward. The more important measure is how does the vision statement live on in thought or in the heart? How does it inspire and motivate action? A high-impact leader leads a vision that is energizing and engaging and becomes a mental picture for everyone—it provokes deep feelings and stirs a sense of possibility and inner commitment.

High-impact leaders possess the will and the desire to go after the vision. They are always striving to hold up and work toward implementing the school's vision. They take every opportunity to share the vision with all stakeholders. They take every opportunity to hold it up and move boldly in whatever forward direction it takes to reach that vision. Their excitement breeds enthusiasm and participation.

The high-impact leader holds a broad view of activity in the school and its vision and uses this information to influence and support the energy in the school. Such a leader also takes the time to develop a deep understanding of purpose among the school community that is strong enough so that the majority of teachers can extend it on their own.

In high-impact schools, the envisioned future is a powerful way to stimulate progress. The vision is cohesive, providing a common thread through the school's mission and subsequent strategies. It is clear and compelling and serves as a unifying focal point of effort. It is inspiring, aiming at excellence as defined by the school. It also describes the core values strongly held by members of the school. It acts as a catalyst for team spirit and it has a clear finish line. It provides a yardstick by which to judge the future performance of the school. According to Saphier and D'Auria (1993, p. 3), "A core value is a central belief deeply understood and shared by every member of an organization. Core values guide the actions of everyone in the organization; they focus its energy and are the anchor points for all its plans."

Creating a Mission—
Providing a Sense of Purpose

High-impact leaders are all about purpose. Purpose creates consensus, commitment, and collegiality. They focus on what is important. They are about what the school needs to achieve. They limit and focus innovations—believing in doing a few things well—quality not quantity. They provide clarity and a sense of shared destiny, hope, and security. Clarity reduces overload complexity, and, in turn, develops empowerment and decision making.

In high-impact schools, the mission and vision serve as a common focus, which helps define the many tasks of establishing a new culture for relationships and responsibility in a school community. Ideally, a school's focus runs deep and wide—flexible enough to recognize the professional talents and competencies of each teacher and articulate enough so that it can be acted on throughout the day, every day, permeating the learning environment and communication.

A mission and a vision focused on students' and other stakeholders' expectations provide the quality-driven school with the foundation it needs to shape its communication systems, its organizational and decision-making structures, and its planning and improvement processes. The school earns the trust, confidence, and loyalty of its students and its other stakeholders, including teachers, parents, and community members, by actively developing and regularly employing listening tools essential for gathering and understanding diverse and distinctive perspectives. The school interprets and weighs these expressed needs, preferences, hopes, and requirements to frame ongoing communication, discussion, and refinement of a common mission and vision. Teachers, staff, and administrators integrate this shared focus into their individual work goals and decision-making strategies.

High-impact schools arrive at a common focus deeply shared by all stakeholders. They write a mission and a vision statement— together providing the common focus for the school. This common focus serves as a guide for everyone as they make decisions and plan instruction. High-impact leaders set the expectation that everyone at the school must have a clear understanding of that mission and share the vision for achieving it.

High-impact leaders promote the identified mission and vision, and by their leadership practices keep people focused on the basic core mission. This commitment is communicated through both informal and formal practices and policies. High-impact leaders have a clear sense of direction for their schools that they are able to articulate just as clearly. They form powerful coalitions to support the school's mission and vision.

High-impact leaders align all practices and processes to pre-serve the school's core values, to reinforce its purpose, and to stimulate its continued progress toward its aspirations. They clarify how significant future trends impact the school's mission, vision, and operation. They encourage continual innovation within agreed purposes at all levels. To succeed, learning organizations need to know what they stand for and need to be on the lookout for rela-tionships and opportunities that emerge. It is all about the capacity to continuously learn, change, and grow.

Such leaders create cultures based on shared values and com-munities of practices guided by shared purpose (Barth, 2001). They are always open to ideas to help them improve. The focus is on achieving a shared vision, and all understand their role in achieving the vision. The focus and vision are developed from common beliefs and values, creating a consistent and purposeful direction for all involved.

In high-impact schools, the faculty blends its collective values and beliefs and its knowledge of best practice to create a compelling mission that captures the school's sense of purpose. Teachers develop and maintain a common purpose for the school that is rooted in a deep understanding of the strengths and needs of their students.

The high-impact leader knows that how the school looks and "feels" communicates a great deal about its mission. Everything about the school directs students toward high levels of perfor-mance, and to achievement beyond. For example, in addition to a nameplate that lists the teacher's name, grade and subject by the door of each teacher's classroom, information regarding the name of the college from which the teacher graduated, the city in which the college is located, and the degree the teacher earned at the col-lege could also be posted. In addition, the walls of the school could be covered with students' work such as science and history projects, creative writing pieces, solved math problems, and other examples of student products. Just by walking down the halls, students know that the school is serious about achievement, and that their work really counts.

High-impact leaders collaboratively develop school mission, beliefs, and vision with involvement of all stakeholder groups. These fundamental tenets are based on deeply held beliefs that give purpose to the work. There is clear, explicit definition and mutual agreement on the purpose of school. The high-impact leader's role in defining the mission involves framing schoolwide goals and communicating these goals in a persistent fashion to the entire school community. At the center of this work to improve their schools are people willing to share their hearts as well as their minds in collective, purposeful action.

Beliefs, Values, and Philosophy— Provides the "Rightness" of the Vision

High-impact leaders ask themselves, "What beliefs define our purpose?" and "How will we know them when we see them?"

High-impact leaders are driven by a set of core values that influence leadership behavior. They have a strong sense of ethics, a clear and powerful vision, and a sincere belief in others. They model the values that define and advance the school's mission. They build their vision around purpose, values, and beliefs—and transform a school from an organization into a community, which inspires the kinds of commitment, devotion, and service that can make schools great.

High-impact leaders have a philosophy and a set of beliefs that provide goals, objectives, and an agenda for school success. They get at the vision. They build trust that leads to the creation of a vision and the building of a covenant that brings together the whole-school community to honor shared values, goals, and beliefs. They understand that the core values of the school are the most important fundamental element of a great, enduring school.

In high-impact schools, the purpose is to optimize student achievement and the core beliefs define that achievement. There is a collective shift in concepts, attitudes, and behaviors that leads to a more effective learning environment. There is an active belief system that defines the actions, thinking, and behaviors that drive everyone to improve the performance of individual students. There is an agreed-upon philosophy, vision, and purpose for all to work within. Core values and principles to which the school aspires organizationally underlie all of the school's activities and processes. This framework must be tight enough to give security, but loose enough to encourage teacher individuality and creativity.

High-impact leaders help school members get clear about core values, rally together in pursuit of improved performance, and strengthen skills. These leaders challenge current conditions. They adapt so that everything is judged according to the school-shared beliefs and vision. They say "No" when necessary; they control their change agenda.

High-impact leaders spread optimism. They manage the heart. They model the way, and they set an example by living their values. They are seen as trustworthy. They live up to their own beliefs and practice what they preach. High-impact leaders treat people and schools with equity, dignity, and respect. They model their values in words and deeds.

In high-impact schools, core values are clearly defined, for without this stake in the ground, there can be no shared vision. Core values are timeless and do not change, while practices and strategies are changing all the time. Unfortunately, some schools cling doggedly to practices that are, in truth, nothing more than familiar habits. As a result, these schools fail to change things that ought to change.

High-impact leaders believe that all students can learn and will respond positively to high expectations. They continuously work to better the way their schools improve, and therefore, provide students with thorough and effective learning opportunities. High-impact leaders continually examine and reflect on their beliefs and practices when it comes to their school's obligations to their students and the community.

The Work of School Improvement

High-impact schools shape the future for our students. They create a plan of action to achieve the school's vision. They have a clear understanding of where their efforts will lead. The plan contains a set of clearly defined and sound strategies the school will utilize to get there. High-impact leaders demonstrate a clear understanding of who the stakeholders are, and they clearly demonstrate their commitment to the distribution and focus of accountability

High-impact leaders are able to clearly and succinctly describe the vision of the school, driving the need for improved performance. They go to the people of the school with a blank slate and conduct purposeful forums to ask some powerful questions about the needs of learners for the twenty-first century. They lead teacher talk about beliefs, vision, mission, student work, and student outcomes. In this way, members shift their roles from writers to researchers and investigators. By bringing more people into the act of inventing and setting the direction for the future, schools see stronger results.

In high-impact schools, school improvement planning, evaluation, and analysis are parts of a unified process. Successful school improvement requires establishing a clear educational vision and a shared institutional mission, knowing how well the school is accomplishing that mission, identifying areas for improvement, developing plans to change educational activities and programs, and implementing those plans or new programs effectively.

In high-impact schools, everyone works together to develop, implement, and monitor school improvement efforts and to form a vision of change over time. These schools have a living school improvement plan to direct actions in both the short and long term. They create student-centered learning environments that continually self-assess their work. They regularly engage in discussion to determine if they are on target for achieving their goals. For example, principals ask, "Where are we moving as a school? How do we know if we are making progress?" Using evidence available in the school to inform their conversations helps them understand their strengths and weaknesses, and perhaps more importantly, helps refine a vision for the kind of school that teachers, parents, and community members want for their students. High-impact schools determine the extent to which their school matches up to the ideal as defined by the school's vision. After conducting this analysis, priorities for improvement are identified, and the school community members maintain a strong commitment to making great strides in their efforts to improve.

High-impact leaders set the stage for school development work by imagining, envisioning, and looking at the current reality from a variety of perspectives. They gather information and options from the collected knowledge and experience of the members of the school community. This becomes the starting point for the heart of school improvement and growth—designing and mapping the action steps. Determining how to go about building and improving the school's capacity to accomplish what has been imagined and envisioned requires thoughtful and thorough discussion. The next step is the building phase, which requires scaffolding support to meet the needs of the development effort. The final step is the review phase where continual monitoring for the actions takes place in order to refine, revise, and improve.

High-impact leaders plan for short-term wins. This provides evidence that sacrifices are worth the effort. After a lot of hard work, positive feedback builds morale and motivation. Short-term wins also give the guiding coalition concrete data on the viability of their ideas. It also helps deny the resistors who want to undermine the changes. Clear improvements in performance make it difficult for people to block needed change.

High-impact leaders engage in a detailed planning process that involves both internal and external stakeholders. They facilitate extended discussions about the school and efforts to improve it, and they make important decisions to support such improvements. They create and plan for visible performance improvements, and they regularly evaluate the progress of the improvement efforts, establish benchmarks for performance, and update plans on the basis of these evaluations. They make the plans work for the school.

Such leaders forge and advocate a vision for school improvement. They act as managers of school improvement, driving the reform process, cultivating the school vision, and using student assessment data to focus on school improvement. They work closely with teachers to develop and monitor progress toward a comprehensive and coherent plan for school improvement. School improvement plans help principals ensure that strategies are aligned with goals and that practices are implemented as designed. High-impact leaders follow up on goals to make sure they are being implemented and working.

Leaders like these not only have a clear vision for the school, but also have a plan in place to make sure that the vision is understood and carried out over time. With improved student learning as the goal, high-impact leaders are able to develop a clear and specific plan to chart the course to achieving the vision. They institutionalize new approaches. The plan has regular monitoring and evaluation benchmarks and is open to revision and modifications as needed. For example, these principals make time to engage in conversations with teachers regarding the level of implementation of school improvement action steps and the impact on student achievement. They regularly ask questions such as, "What successes are you having in your classroom? What evidence do you have to support your thoughts? What are you doing to promote school improvement and raise student achievement? What needs to be done differently?"

In high-impact schools, the vision serves as a sensible and appealing picture of the future. Strategies provide the logic for how the vision can be achieved. The plan describes the specific steps and outlines a timetable to implement the strategies. The improvement activities are directly related to the target in ways that will result in significant improvement and these activities are powerful enough to result in the desired improvement. High-impact leaders engage in a school improvement process that results in positive changes in people, processes, and systems that in turn cause positive changes in student performance.

Current Reality—What's Working?

High-impact leaders look at a comprehensive picture of student learning. They conduct an inventory of the schools' performance through a systematic gathering of data to develop a school profile. The need for the profile is based on the premise that a school must have a clear picture of its current status, or "what is," before effective changes can be made. The greater the diversity of the information sources, the greater the credibility of the picture.

Once information is collected, it is organized and analyzed in order to create viable information that can be used to identify gaps between current performance and the desired performance of the schools' students. Both strengths and weaknesses are examined. Strengths can often be used in developing strategies to help improve weaknesses, and successful strategies in one area may be replicated in another.

High-impact leaders often ask "why" and "what if" questions. The right questions force people to examine underlying assumptions and consider new possibilities. However, to get the feedback they need, schools must demonstrate a high degree of openness and trust. For example, a principal might lead a discussion to identify what are the key factors that determine school success. Teachers brainstorm these ideas and create a list of the activities that are important to producing positive results in their school. Next, they identify the current level of success in each of these areas by placing sticky dots on the list under a rating scale. This provides immediate feedback of where the school is with respect to best practice. This sets the stage for defining the school's current reality.

High-impact leaders also look for barriers to school success. They look around the school, talking to teachers, students, and parents, getting input and asking, "If these are our core values and this is fundamentally why we exist, what are the obstacles that get in our way? What barriers inhibit learning improvement?" In other words, what policies and practices that may obscure the school's underlying values have become institutionalized? These leaders regularly survey what's working and what's not.

An educational leader's success hinges on his ability to mobilize the school in such a way that the gap between current reality and a powerful vision for the future is significantly diminished. This strategic work calls not only for the building of a shared vision and effectively communicating that vision, but it also involves clarifying and communicating the stark facts of current reality. If the picture of the current reality is honest and if the vision is clear and powerful, the distance between the two may be significant. And that gap between vision and current reality serves as the source for the change—it creates dissatisfaction with the status quo and creates the urgency to move forward.

Data-Enriched Thinking

School improvement efforts are most successful when they are based on research and when the decision-making process is data-driven. High-impact schools collect, analyze, and use data as a basis for making decisions. They grapple with school-generated assessment data to identify areas for more extensive and intensive improvement. The high-impact school delineates benchmarks and insists on evidence and results. It intentionally and explicitly reconsiders its vision and practices when data-based questions arise.

High-impact schools seek and use data and information to assess current capacities and to measure performance realistically. The whole staff tracks progress concretely and consistently, and uses performance results to set ambitious but attainable targets that increase and improve the school's capability to meet its students' needs and expectations. The school develops and refines systems for gathering and assessing valuable feedback and data and continuously seeks better methods for obtaining the most useful information on which to base decisions and improvements.

Examining the school's belief system and asking the right questions must be augmented by the collection, analysis, and interpretation of data. High-impact schools use data to determine the gaps between what they believe and what they do (Robison, Stemple, & McCree, 2005). Data is used as a formative assessment rather than summative assessment. School interventions and adjustments are made in response to intermittent data review. The question is "How do we close those gaps?" In high-impact schools, good enough is neither good nor is it enough. The data doesn't lie. If you have a lower performing group, you have the data, and you develop a strategy. For example, these principals will use data as a means for planning rather than just describing the past.

The quality education process is only effective when teams find the root cause of problems. This means digging deep in the data to get at the "why" of the problem. Data provides the rationale for making the right decisions. To learn something, you must first have enough information to understand it. However, school faculties are flooded with data—high-impact leaders must assist teacher teams in turning data into information and disseminating the information to everyone throughout the school. Compiling, tracking, and reporting data will continue to grow in importance as schools' accountability to the public increases. Schools are compelled to gather and disseminate data accurately and responsibly. High-impact leaders recognize the value of data to the success of the schools' improvement efforts.

High-impact leaders engage in the continuous use of data, not only to monitor student performance but also to target the needs of students and teachers and to uncover instructional areas requiring improvement. Data provides the first clue that there is a problem

(Schmoker, 1999). Such leaders look for movement—they pull data weekly to monitor the progress of the school. They take this information and provide leadership, resources, and training to implement change where it is needed. In high-impact schools, it is clear that data is a primary driver for decisions relating to academic improvement.

Strategic Planning—Identifying Priorities

High-impact leaders develop plans that include priorities for action. These priorities are based on the analysis of data in the school profile, and they are followed by benchmarks to help assess progress toward the priorities. Plans are subsequently revised to improve on weaknesses and to build on strengths. A constant, consistent, critical focus is maintained. Are we strengthening school operations? Is teaching improving? Are students learning more? Such strategic planning depends on the school's ability to look at evidence about itself, to analyze it critically, and to respond to the greatest needs with a plan.

High-impact leaders help people see the big picture—they connect day-to-day learning events with the school's mission, vision, and key strategies. They encourage teacher participation and creativity. They provide opportunities that broaden teachers' understanding of how all pieces of the school puzzle fit together. They make special projects and experiences available that will provide opportunities for gaining new insights and skills.

In high-impact schools, there is a sense of what its members are working toward. There is strong program coherence, which supports alignment of programs and activities for school improvement. High-impact schools develop action plans detailing intentional development efforts. Within these schools, educational priorities are evident.

High-impact leaders are able to describe a future that is better in some important way. They reconsider the impact of growing knowledge bases about teaching, learning, and leadership through the lenses of mission and vision. A clear and compelling vision challenges people to think and act differently as they pursue a new agenda. The leaders of these schools guide, escort, and illuminate the pathways to school success.

These leaders have a strong set of personal core values and a relentless drive for progress with a remarkable ability to translate visions into concrete actions. They begin by addressing a few highly visible problems that can be resolved quickly. This shows teachers that they are serious about making necessary changes.

Many schools plan more than they could ever implement, monitor, or evaluate, and, consequently, a lot of time and energy is wasted trying to do so. All this wasted time and energy might have been better used to focus on teaching and learning; more success might have been realized by doing fewer things well and encouraging teachers to focus on improvement by a few key actions. High-impact leaders prioritize initiatives and identify precisely what will have the most impact.

These leaders have sources of inner direction that give them a sturdy guide for planning and action (Elmore, 2000). They encourage the search for new ideas that might help the school improve student learning, and they are also willing to challenge the status quo to implement them. They articulate a vision for improvement and hold high standards for all. They place students and their well-being at the center of school decisions. High-impact leaders strive with pride and commitment to have world-class schools.

Establishing Shared Goals and Objectives

High-impact schools have challenging but achievable and shared goals. These goals are demanding, but they actually guide the organization and gain the dedication of teachers and other members of the school community. High-impact schools develop collective autonomy or shared responsibility as members of the school collaborate in pursuit of shared goals and interests that serve both the individual and the school. According to Lemahieu (1997, p. 583), "The principal's new role [has become] that of organizational leader; developing consensus, facilitating collaborative problem solving and managing collective action." The high-impact school is a unified system in its determination to achieve the desired outcomes while fostering inquiry and creativity.

Meaningful reflection and discussion is encouraged to help develop shared goals for school improvement. Goals are based on the assessment of students' needs. The community of adults and students within the school has established goals that drive all decisions and create conditions unique to the school. In high-impact schools, staff and students consistently express common beliefs and values.

There is a clear and shared focus that captures the imagination and enthusiasm of members of the school. There are specific goals that focus attention, effort, and resources. To effectively prioritize a specific focus, high-impact leaders use collaborative processes to target one or two areas as school goals and then build consensus around them. These schools succeed in establishing a goal that resonates with the school community members.

High-impact leaders are visible in the school and demonstrate their interest in instruction. They have high expectations for all students and are focused on learning goals. For example, they ask, "What do you know about your students? How are they learning? What engages them? How do you work with students who are struggling? What support can I provide?" They inspire teachers to go beyond the expected. The principal's actions, commitment, and relentless dedication to the school make students, faculty, and staff feel inspired to go the extra mile.

The leaders of these schools possess and cultivate the collective will to persevere and to overcome barriers. They believe it is their responsibility to produce increased achievement and enhanced development for all students. They communicate the importance of the learning goals through consistent messages, asking students, "What are you learning?" or "What have you read?" Accountability for meeting student goals is present, and incentives for doing so are in place. High-impact schools believe that the schoolwide goals can be reached.

Leading Change for Continuous Quality Improvement and Development

High-impact leaders are able to establish in others a sense of urgency to achieve at higher levels. They create a burning platform for change. These principals are sensitive to the needs of their teachers and work toward empowering their followers to make things happen in the school. They use a strengths-based approach so that the change is institutionalized. For example, they highlight the individual strengths and talents of the faculty to emphasize the potential of success and achievement. They act on the collective professional knowledge to inspire and motivate change.

High-impact leaders use the school's vision to help direct the change effort. The vision says something that clarifies the direction in which the school needs to move. High-impact leaders develop strategies for achieving that vision. The vision magnetically pulls all parts of the organization together.

In high-impact schools, there is a common focus on creating a significantly improved learning environment for students. This focus leads to substantial improvement in the performance of everyone in the school community. Core values and purpose remain fixed while practices, strategies, structures, systems, policies, and procedures are open for change.

High-impact schools research the strategies that are right for their context, make thoughtful decisions about what needs to change, and then stay the course. Long-term commitments to the change initiative help teachers internalize change and move improvement forward. A shared vision of what a high-impact school is and does drives every facet of school change.

High-impact leaders focus on long-term changes to the teaching and learning core. These leaders ask, "How is student performance impacted by our changes in strategies and the way we do our work?" They make the system changes that promote best practices, provide targeted professional development, and manage the myriad day-to-day decisions that must be made to maximize instructional time and resources for student learning.

High-impact leaders plan and manage change in a dynamic organization. They generate a sense of urgency for improving the school's performance. They celebrate what's right with schools and energize schools for student success. For example, they ask, "What has made us effective? What would enable us to stay effective?" Principals in these schools spend time discussing what effective practice actually looks like so that it becomes an agreed-upon concept. In this way, everyone understands what effective performance looks like and what needs to be done. This helps to consolidate improvements and produce more change.

High-impact schools anchor change in a new culture. Expectations of continuous improvement permeate the school. The common focus is used to drive needed changes. These principals actively seek feedback on all aspects of the school improvement work. They ask, "What is working? What is not? What needs to be done differently?" They use forums, focus groups, surveys, etc., to generate the conversations that build a culture where the habit of continually asking how can we get better becomes the norm.

High-impact leaders develop a sufficient climate of understanding so that all the people who work in the school care about the institution and identify with its destiny. They lead by example, with their actions, their conversations, their beliefs, and their respect for all who are involved in the school. They create a "transformational agenda" based on innovation and inquiry.

High-impact leaders build a collaborative school culture that supports change and innovation. They facilitate collegiality and experimentation with trust, confidence, and high expectations. They protect what's important. They integrate research-based leadership and transform management principles into the leadership culture of the school.

Leaders like these are serious, really serious about student performance. They set high standards for everyone in the school including themselves. They don't give up. The work is demanding and challenging, but the rewards are great with students. There are no easy fixes. Growth takes time. There is no secret formula. High-impact leaders sometimes have to move the boulder slowly.

The outlook of a high-impact school is a future focus. Leaders must think about what the school will have to look like in the years to come in order to serve its clients of the future. High-impact schools improve themselves through their collective will. This provides students with the opportunity to achieve beyond previous expectations.

High-impact schools are more reflective and deliberative than other schools. However, with the rapid development of new knowledge and technologies, and with the rising expectations of community stakeholders, high-impact schools must also develop flexibility to respond quickly to the changing needs of a growing population that is becoming more diverse every day.

Such schools think into the future, tracking trends in order to better predict how conditions will change, and anticipating how these changes may affect students. Foresight enables these schools to innovate and to make meaningful changes to improve their services and processes in ways that create new or added value for students and other stakeholders. While they remain open to new approaches and techniques, these schools design, test, and improve their planning structures and processes through practical use and experience.

High-impact schools see mandates for school change and improvement as opportunities. No longer is the question, "Will we change our schools?"; instead, the question is, "How willing are we to invest necessary time and energy, and what risks are we willing to take for our students?"

High-impact schools focus on the changes they can make. They direct their energies to the actions that will move their kids forward. They don't settle for "good enough" work; they hold high expectations.

High-impact leaders listen to the heartbeat of the school, and their schools become stronger and more resilient. They regularly "dip-stick" by being visible on campus, by talking and listening, and by looking around. These activities increase the understanding of how the school is working, and more importantly whether it is working well or in some cases, it is not. Leadership inevitably involves change and change inevitably involves learning.

Requisite Leadership— Provides Focus, Courage, and Encouragement

Schools can be more successful and can have greater impact, but there's no getting there without visionary leadership. High-impact leaders create school cultures that enable thriving. They are the architects of positive culture. These leaders create learning cultures around learning principles. They are models of what is expected and what to expect. High-impact leaders set high expectations for themselves, for their staff, and for all students. They set and articulate their own learning goals, demonstrating the need for continuous learning. They are mindful of the big picture, and they bring current research and high standards to the discussion on sound educational practice.

In high-impact schools, the principal displays facilitative leadership by encouraging broad participation in decision making, school improvements, and increased student academic performance. These leaders help people feel significant; they let others know that they make a difference. They empower the people within the school to do the work and then protect those people from unwarranted outside interference.

High-impact leadership requires proximity and visibility. High-impact leaders wander about the school and into the surrounding community, listening and learning, asking questions, building relationships, and identifying possibilities. High-impact leaders shift from a top-down leader to become a facilitator, an architect, a steward, an instructional leader, a coach, and a strategic teacher. Such a leader succeeds only to the extent that he or she empowers teachers and students to succeed.

Trust drives the working relationships. High-impact leaders honestly appraise whether they genuinely trust and value teacher participation in the school's operation and whether commitment to their involvement is a priority. The underlying attitudes and commitments reflected in these dynamics determine whether any specific form of shared leadership is effective or ineffective, extensive or limited, meaningful or superficial.

High-impact leaders encourage the heart. They recognize that achieving extraordinary things takes hard work. They recognize contributions, celebrate accomplishments, and share accolades. They make people feel like heroes.

Visionary leadership is a critical component of high-impact schools. Their leaders are purposeful in their choices and actions. They bring as many people as possible into the process and use their ideas to create a powerful, shared vision for the future. They create standards of excellence and set the example for others. High-impact principals are thoughtful about connecting with all teachers in the school.

High-impact leaders set and communicate the direction for a student-focused, learning-oriented environment to guide the activities and decisions of the school. They involve all stakeholders in creating the vision, mission, and expectations for the school. They participate and support actively in the development and alignment of processes, systems, and strategies for continuous improvement and performance excellence. They stimulate innovation and build capacity throughout the school. They take responsibility for the vision, mission, values, expectations, and performance of the school. A web of common values permeates high-impact schools that have a systematic approach to continuous quality improvement. High-impact leaders create a sense of urgency to achieve the school's mission.

High Impact Leadership: Improving Practice
Self-Assessment Tool

It's About the Mission!	Absent	Developing	Good	Exemplary
We know our fundamental reason for existence.				
We share a common set of core values.				
Our mission is clear and unites us all.				
We know what we want our school to look like in the future.				
There is evidence that the mission, values, and beliefs are acted on by teachers and staff.				
I have created and maintained a vision for the school that is supported by members of the school community.				
We have performed a formal comprehensive analysis of our school around areas such as student performance, school community, professional development, school climate, curriculum and instructional practices, resource allocation, etc.				
We have created goals, objectives, and priorities for our school and actively maintain urgency in meeting them.				
The School Improvement Plan guides our daily activities and instructional decisions.				
All the people in the school know what the schoolwide goals are and their personal responsibility in helping achieve them.				
I solicit teacher, student, parent input on a regular basis (e.g., through conversations, surveys, etc.) for decision making.				

Next Steps ... REFLECTION and ACTION!

It's About the Mission, Not the Mission Statement

♦ What do I do each and every day to achieve our school vision?

♦ Strengths? (Good and Exemplary Practices)

♦ Challenges? (Absent or Developing Practices)

♦ What actions will I take to better move our school forward to achieve the school vision?

♦ What should we celebrate and how?

Chapter 2

High Expectations for Each and Every Student

The price of greatness is responsibility.

—Winston Churchill

In high-impact schools, teachers engage students in a learning process that maximizes excellence and equity. Because teachers make no assumptions about why students cannot learn, no self-fulfilling prophecies prevail. Principals must focus on a learning agenda that ensures a rigorous standard of student performance and must provide the needed supports for students to succeed.

High-Impact Leaders Ask:

♦ How do we ensure that we keep student achievement as a focus of our school practices? Have we organized all of our efforts around making sure that every student progresses?

♦ Is it glaringly apparent that everyone has high expectations for the education process and values each person in the school? Have we kept our goals high?

♦ Are we focusing on what we can do something about rather than complaining about those things we can't?

♦ Is there a shared sense of accountability? Does everyone know what criteria they have to live up to—how success is to be judged?

♦ Does our school climate help students feel they belong in the school community? Do our students feel they are respected and their heritage and background are viewed as positive, not detrimental to the learning community?

Raising the Bar—Collective Responsibility

High-impact leaders promote an academic learning climate. They ensure that all students reach the level of academic achievement that was once expected of only a few. Considerations of both excellence and equity guide every decision they make. High-impact leaders make high expectations part of the way they do business; they expect excellence, monitor performance, and provide feedback as necessary. A no-excuses mentality permeates the culture of the school they lead (Johnson & Asera, 1999). These leaders engage in regular conversation to ask, "How do we communicate high expectations for student performance and let our students know that we believe them all to be capable of success? How do we communicate caring and interest to students and that no one is expected to fail?"

In high-impact schools, the vision impacts expectations and demeanor in ways you can feel walking the halls. Academic success of all students is the school's mission and all efforts are organized around making sure that every student progresses. Teachers form a strong team and take active steps to create a family atmosphere in the school. They value their students. They embrace the premise that the very reason their school exists is to help each and every one of their students to acquire the essential knowledge and skills needed for success.

In high-impact schools, everyone is part of the solution. A job title does not matter as much as does one's potential to contribute. Teachers at all grade levels, in both regular and special programs of all content areas, as well as professional support personnel (counselors, nurses, librarians, and psychologists) and support staff (instructional aides, office staff, custodians, bus drivers, and cafeteria workers) are all enlisted to be a part of the team that leads to student success. Everyone unites on behalf of students.

Schools such as these build a consistent school culture among adults and students that models and reinforces personal responsibility and aspiration to achieve excellence as individuals and as a school community. There is a focus on continuous improvement along with positive and explicit social norms. There is a system that supports challenging, rigorous and direct feedback within a safe environment. Personal engagement and positive relationships that enable learning from others is encouraged (Flanary, 2005).

High-impact schools are compelled by a common belief that they can collectively impact the learning of all students. They make an intentional and deliberate effort to establish and practice group norms regarding expectations for students. There is a sense that the school focuses on the student as a person. There is the belief that every child can learn at high levels. Success is expected of all students.

High-impact leaders ensure that the focus of educational programs is on high student achievement supported by high expectations. They engage in a process to significantly and rapidly improve academic performance for students. They support, motivate, and intensify the school's efforts to provide effective instructional opportunities and options for each student. They are able to remove barriers and low expectations that often prevent schools from moving past incremental improvement goals.

In high-impact schools, a common focus on high expectations drives the creation and ongoing renewal of a unique culture, which serves as the platform for significant shifts in both attitudes and actions. As a result, cohesiveness emerges from within the school, as it becomes a learning community where everyone plays a different role. The focus on a high-quality education for every student becomes more robust, evolving organically as a shared idea.

In these schools, there is a common view on important academic issues. Teachers and administrators alike agree on what the academic goals of the school are, and they are able to describe what they are doing to achieve these goals. They assume the responsibility for the success of students and identify measures of such success.

High-impact leaders help people become more and achieve more than they ever thought possible. They stretch people beyond the boundaries they had set for themselves. They make a commitment to cultivate a trusting relationship with teachers. As a result, teachers feel collectively responsible for children. They believe they can succeed with any student regardless of the student's previous difficulties or challenges. High-impact leaders encourage teachers to not accept difficult situations as reasons to lower academic expectations. Instead, the teachers seek ways to overcome these issues and experiment with creative solutions so that every student can excel.

In high-impact schools there is a common focus on success for every student. For opportunity to become reality, schools must have a shared vision. Everyone in a high-impact school works together toward achieving a common goal, motivated by shared values and principles. All are on the path toward high achievement for all. They are optimistic that their practices will lead to a better education for all students. The expectation is excellence.

Shared Accountability—Clarity of Expectations

Schools face new and different challenges when trying to help all students achieve. However, high-impact leaders hold teachers accountable for high expectations. These expectations are encouraged through fostering shared beliefs and values, having clear goals, and leading with a shared vision of change.

High-impact leaders always expect the best—they expect everyone to continuously improve and sincerely believe that improvement will take place. They ensure that all understand what criteria they have to live up to—how success is to be judged. They listen attentively and follow through on commitments; they enable others to act by clarifying expectations and by building trust. They build commitment by keeping their word and respecting the views of others.

In high-impact schools, there is a culture infused with responsibility. Everyone takes ownership of student performance and student accomplishments are proudly displayed. Each person believes that the academic success for all students depends on everyone knowing what can be accomplished and how. Collectively, they see their responsibility as ensuring that no child slips through unprepared to pursue a productive life. They set the bar higher for each student, and they work together to make sure everyone clears his bar. Together, their efforts add up.

A high-impact school holds itself accountable for its students' success rather than blaming others for its shortcomings. Teachers actively participate in the development of the school. The idea of collective responsibility does not relieve individuals of personal or professional responsibility, but instead focuses that responsibility on efforts to ensure progress.

Resourceful leadership, outside-the-box thinking, and bold determination make a clear and remarkable difference. High-impact leaders promote the spirit of success for each and every student. They communicate the need to dramatically increase student achievement using creative, results-oriented approaches and techniques to better educate children. They stress the importance of paralleling high expectations for children with high expectations for teachers. Teachers are expected to continue to learn, inquire, experiment, and be reflective.

In high-impact schools, trust and honesty are the foundation of all individual and school efforts. Teachers and staff members value doing the right thing and are accountable for their actions even when no one is watching. High expectations lead to better performance by students, teachers, and everyone else.

In high-impact schools there is a shared culture within the school that values improving student achievement and assumes responsibility for it (Marriott, 2001). These schools have well-defined plans for instructional improvement. They make meeting the state and federal accountability goals a priority, and they set measurable goals that exceed the mandated targets. They embrace external expectations as indicators of their progress.

High-impact leaders are vigilant about holding everyone accountable for student success. They do so by continuously collecting and interpreting the data available on student achievement. They want to know, on a daily basis, how students are performing, why they are performing well or not so well, and how the school can help students perform at higher levels. They use this information to identify the practices that enhance chances for success and to isolate those that impede or close the doors to success.

High-impact leaders are clear about their expectations for meeting school goals. They hold people accountable to agreed-upon commitments—even when they know it would be easier to ignore those commitments. High-impact leaders show moral toughness. They are tenacious and see conflict as an opportunity. They stay the course to allow change to occur so that new practices become institutionalized and lasting. They have an overriding commitment to their students.

Equity and Excellence

In high-impact schools, all children are provided an equal chance to succeed. This represents the best and most enduring part of the American Dream, as education has always been tied to the promise of equality and opportunity for all.

The guiding question for high-impact schools is, "What will it take to create a school where every student, regardless of the level of his existing academic performance, can expect to succeed?"

The leaders of high-impact schools organize themselves around the belief that all students can and will learn. They provide every student with a learning environment that nurtures the student's individual gifts and talents. The aim is clear; each and every student will be provided access to an education that helps him achieve his highest ability and realize his full potential.

High-impact leaders keep everyone's focus on the larger vision, ensuring that there are equitable opportunities for every student. These leaders strive to enable every student in the school to be successful, and they hold high academic goals for each one. The principal works to harness all the school's physical, financial, and human resources so that every student benefits. They ensure that the school's policies and practices do not privilege some students while alienating others. High-impact leaders constantly reflect on and critique their schools' processes to ensure equitable treatment and outcomes for every student.

High-impact schools have a deep-seated belief in the capability of each and every student to learn and achieve (Dougherty, 2006). Teachers have high expectations for every child, and they focus on the belief that every child will learn. By raising expectations far beyond the limits others have placed on students, teachers can take those students to higher levels than previously imagined.

Schools promote engagement when they raise their expectations for student conduct and achievement. Every student needs and deserves the support and inspiration conveyed by high expectations. High-impact schools do more that just profess that "all children can learn." They put expectations into actions so that all children do learn. When a school acts on high expectations, it creates a climate where academics are emphasized. The school sends a strong message that academic work is important and valued. Individual learning needs are targeted for attention, rather than categorizing students as part of an at-risk group held to different performance expectations. Engaging in significant intellectual work is a driving core value that serves as a filter for learning choices and decision making.

High-impact schools focus on discovering the skills and meeting the needs of every student. There is the pursuit of rigorous course content across a broad range of academic levels. All students have equal access to valued knowledge in all school classes and activities. High expectations are communicated to students characterized as "average" or "below average," and aggressive efforts are made to place borderline students in more challenging classes (Quick & Quick, 2000).

High-impact schools provide the time, instruction, resources, and encouragement necessary to provide equitable opportunities, and therefore help struggling students achieve. These schools provide learning activities and materials that are at least as interesting and varied as those provided to other students. In high-impact schools, all students are engaged in challenging and interesting academic work.

High-impact leaders examine school data to ensure that there is not a disproportionate representation of poor students or minority students who are impacted by particular school policies or who are found in specialized learning environments. High-impact leaders ask, for example, which students are in special education classes? Which are in remedial classes? Which are in gifted classes? Are certain groups of student underrepresented in some classes and overrepresented in other classes? High-impact leaders look at class counts that are disaggregated by subgroups. They ask, "Who is getting suspended or expelled?" They examine both attendance numbers and rates of discipline actions to ensure that there are fair and consistent opportunities for every student to succeed. Such leaders ensure that their schools are not failing minority and/or poor students. They ensure that equity is always considered in determining access to educational opportunities and experiences.

The Motto of High-Impact Leaders:
When you believe they can do it, they rise to the challenge.

Climate of Care

High-impact leaders create a school that fosters belonging. In high-impact schools, teachers communicate high expectations for student performance. They tell students that they believe in them and that they are capable of learning and achieving. No one is expected to fail. In these schools, as students arrive for the day, the principal meets them at the front door and acknowledges them with a smile or a comment about school assignments or after-school activity. The regular greeting of the students tells them that they belong in this school and they are safe and cared for.

High-impact schools encourage effort, focusing on the positive aspects of students' work and behavior. They have moved beyond thinking about the deficits of children to thinking about the strengths of children; they view children as learners. They create a supportive learning environment where students are engaged in learning because they feel respected and connected with teachers.

High-impact schools believe deeply in the potential of their students. In these schools, persistence and faith provide the means by which students reach success. Leaders of high-impact schools believe that it is their responsibility to prepare students for success after school and to ensure that students have choices and options for achievement. This may necessitate changes in scheduling, classroom structure, and use of staff. Vigorous attention is paid to developing student skills; workshops and afterschool programs provide extra support for students who struggle. Leaders of high-impact schools create an orderly and positive environment for student learning and address such areas as attendance policies, rule enforcement and respect for cultural differences.

In high-impact schools, the culture and climate foster student resiliency. They engage students emotionally, intellectually, and socially. They believe in students and acknowledge every learning effort. These schools focus on students' strengths and establish protective factors that help students learn to cope with adverse conditions. They help students overcome setbacks by empowering them to see adversity as temporary and surmountable.

In schools like these, there is constant conversation among all colleagues about how to better achieve the school's purpose. Through collegial conversations, administrators and teachers critically analyze the assumptions that preserve the status quo and interfere with closing the gap between what is and what can be.

Personalization

The signature feature of high-impact schools is a concern for students as individuals. These schools promote students' personal well-being and ensure a supportive context for learning. Teachers press every student to do significant work while providing students needed support through greater personalization and caring.

High-impact schools maintain a climate that is conducive to serious work and learning. In order to achieve this climate, the school must be safe, orderly, and respectful. Everyone works together to uphold agreed-upon standards of appropriate behavior. The rules are upheld in a fair and humane manner that focuses on developing each student's sense of responsibility to himself and to his peers. Praise and recognition of positive behavior is evident.

High-impact schools develop a learning structure that accommodates students, learning styles, and natural talents and interests. These schools understand that students are not standardized and that teaching is not routine. In these schools, teachers base judgments on knowledge of learning theory and pedagogy, child development, and curriculum and assessment. They then connect this knowledge to the understanding and attitudes that individual students bring with them to the classroom. High-impact teachers see their most important role as providing highly engaging, optimal learning opportunities matched to each student.

In high-impact schools, everyone's energy is focused on meeting the needs of each student, communicating high academic and social expectations, and respecting the richness and value every adult and student bring to the school (Boaler, 2006). All involved look for ways to get at the root of the problems students have, and they implement interventions to help students meet the expectations for their learning. They identify and monitor each student's needs. They make plans to where each student is and where they need to go.

High-impact leaders create a school culture in which the learning community operates to provide a closer personal academic relationship between adults and students. These principals visit classrooms each week to work with students on their attitudes and expectations about learning and education and future opportunities. They form strong relationships with students and provide them with attention that they are not often used to receiving. Attention is focused on developing a climate of respect and responsibility, high expectations, and personalized learning.

Professionalism

High-impact leaders create a supportive atmosphere in which all staff members are expected to be highly competent professionals and to continue their education. A learning ethic permeates the school culture. High-impact leaders develop strategies so that all people work together to build school capacity. High-impact principals recognize that effective administration depends on relationships and shared values between leaders and followers. These principals empower their colleagues.

Trust and professionalism are key elements of the culture in high-impact schools. In such schools, each staff member knows he is an integral part of the whole and understands that he plays a key role in the education of students. Teachers in high-impact schools have lofty intellectual standards and work well with each other in collegial, critical ways. They clearly know what they want of each of the students. They strive to close the gap between conversation about high expectations and the demanding, hard, professional work it takes to truly educate all students.

In high-impact schools, everyone works together in ways that increase the overall learning capacity of the school. All partners productively engage in creating and sustaining a school with student learning as the focus. There is a strong culture of support for students, within which teachers work to ensure high performance for everyone. There is group ownership of the learning process, and teachers are committed to the success of each and every student.

High-impact leaders focus on developing expertise in the school. They define the conditions for creativity. They learn to trust teachers, and they encourage them to reflect and learn from successful experiences. They provide every student with high-quality teachers, resources, learning opportunities and support systems. They keep options open for all students.

Positive interactions among teachers and between teachers and students are hallmarks of high-impact schools. Teachers see each other as resources. The environment is one of personal trust; the school is a place in which everyone has high expectations of everyone else, respect goes both ways, and persistence is a given. Teams and other such structures are in place to promote regular, substantive interaction and communication among teachers. For example, teacher members of learning teams, which consist of four to eight members, assist one another in examining the standards students are expected to achieve, planning more effective lessons, critiquing student work, and solving the common problems of teaching. There is a solid collective ownership of the learning process.

High-impact leaders spend a great deal of time establishing and building strong relationships with teachers and school community members. They delegate responsibilities and provide professional autonomy within the parameters of the mission and vision.

The requirements of high-impact schools include reflection about current practices and common purpose, willingness to entertain new information and perspectives, and mutual trust built on a history of fulfilled commitments and accomplished goals. The culture of professionalism within the school brings staff and community together to use skills successfully to further the school's mission (Donaldson, 2001).

Academic Focus—Monitoring and Accelerating Improvement

In high-impact schools, there is frequent monitoring of teaching and learning to check on the effectiveness of school and classroom practices (Cross & Rice, 2000). A steady cycle of different assessments is used to identify students who need help. Support and instructional time are provided, both during the school day and outside normal school hours, to students who need more help.

High-impact schools go to great lengths to establish a school climate that engages students socially, psychologically, and intellectually. When students invest themselves in learning, they take pride in incorporating new knowledge and skills into their lives. When students are not engaged in schools, they either do not come to school to learn, or they do not come to school at all. High-impact schools strive to develop an engaging and meaningful learning program and to encourage pride in academic success. They cultivate student engagement through changes to their instructional programs and their school climate.

High-impact schools provide the personal and academic support that students need in order to thrive. Structures and processes are created that increase the potential for students to get to know one another well and to build trusting and positive relationships. Students understand that school provides an opportunity to practice for a different and better future.

In schools like these, students are provided opportunities to engage in learning opportunities flexible enough to encompass their varying styles and skills. They try a variety of strategies to help struggling students, such as regrouping students, engaging interns and parents to extend instructional time, and providing intensive assistance outside of the regular school day.

In high-impact schools, students are challenged and supported as they learn increasingly rigorous content and apply their knowledge to real-world contexts. These schools promote active involvement of all students in the learning process and provide opportunities for all students to explore the application of higher-order thinking skills. Students work individually, in small groups, or in animated class discussions. Student presentations are a common sight on any day as students share the products of their enthusiastic learning. Student learning is about performance, where success is recognized by considering the results. These schools regularly investigate new approaches to helping students apply their learning so they can use it meaningfully.

In high-impact schools, a clear curriculum is front and center since it serves as a roadmap of what to teach. A curriculum is offered that challenges each student to excel, reflects a commitment to equity, and demonstrates an appreciation of diversity. Principals and teachers know exactly what is to be taught and learned at each grade and in each subject.

These schools use data systematically to inform the policy, management, and instructional changes that result in higher student achievement for every student. They create a student database to help identify and monitor each student's needs. The data lets high-impact decision makers know if a program is having the effect for which it was instituted or if it is not worth the time and resources expended. Discussions revolve around patterns and trends of the data, with teachers identifying strengths and weaknesses that emerge. Teachers use data for future planning rather than for simply describing or explaining past performance. Highly effective schools collect data to demonstrate verifiable growth in student performance.

In high-impact schools everyone takes responsibility for ensuring that struggling students get the additional help they need early on. They have systems in place to identify students who need help before it's too late. They don't wait until a student fails in order to provide remediation. This helps students stay on track and keeps them motivated to continue. They mandate additional programs for students who are in jeopardy of not passing. They provide the additional support to help students achieve.

In high-impact schools, student achievement is prioritized using measurable and monitored objectives. The schools place importance on setting clear, high, and measurable expectations for student achievement. These expectations are visible in classrooms where teachers provide students with exemplars of high-quality work that meets the performance standard. But it isn't just about expectations—it is about careful instruction to meet those expectations.

In such schools, the learning objectives of the day are posted. The schools measure student achievement with a common assessment every 3 weeks in all grades and core subjects. Teachers are eager to monitor the data they receive regularly on their students, so that they can adjust instruction to keep children on track.

High-impact schools consistently look beyond preparation for the next grade level. Instead, they continuously emphasize increasing rigor to better prepare students for future choices beyond school and graduation. There is steady talk about the importance of getting students into tougher classes to ready them for more postgraduation choices. High-impact decision makers open doors for students to take more rigorous classes. For example, in high school, students are encouraged to try honors or Advanced Placement courses when GPA or other barriers to enrollment are removed.

In these schools there is a focus on student learning, and the instruction is geared toward high expectations and improved academic outcomes for students. Teachers and administrators hold consistent views about achievement and school goals. There is group ownership of the learning process, and teachers are committed to each and every student.

Student-Centered Climate

High-impact schools create a rich teaching and learning environment where every student thrives. They pay attention to students' interests, problems, and accomplishments. Classrooms are warm and inviting, and learning activities are purposeful, engaging, and significant. Teachers express genuine interest and concern for students. As a result, students come to trust that teachers will be honest and fair, and the school climate is positive.

In high-impact schools, students feel they belong in the school community. They feel they are respected, and their heritage and background are viewed as positive, not detrimental to the learning community (Villegas & Lucas, 2007).

High-impact schools demonstrate a sense of deliberate energy focused on helping students succeed. These schools find ways to support struggling students by whatever means are necessary. Students are encouraged to self-monitor their progress. They graph their achievement on a chart that lists all of the standards they are expected to learn. Once they have mastered a particular standard, they mark the box next to the standard they have completed. This allows students to take responsibility for mastering standards while allowing teachers to see which standards need to be retaught. Teachers meet individually with students to discuss their performance and analyze their progress. Teachers also create class charts with class progress noted on individual standards. This public presentation of student achievement leads to discussion about successes and challenges and reinforces student and teacher accountability. In high-impact schools, there are no secrets about student performance.

High-impact schools provide all students with guidance on learning beyond the expectations they have of themselves. Even when it seems that students don't have any expectations of themselves, high-impact schools find ways to get successful results. These dramatic improvements occur because of an active belief system that every student is highly capable and these capabilities need only to be uncovered.

In high-impact schools, teachers use instructional practices that demonstrate their belief in the students. These practices also reflect teachers' belief in their ability to teach students to high standards, and their persistence in teaching them. High-impact schools challenge all students to use their minds well. They teach for understanding so that students can achieve at high levels.

High-impact leaders establish schools with a spirit and culture that pulsate. The defining factor is respect and trust—how the adults work with students and each other and the expectations they set. They intentionally develop a school culture that is supportive of and serves as a commonly understood driver of the overall climate in the school. When a school culture is highly refined, students are actively engaged, adults make better use of their time, and the atmosphere throughout the school is positive. There is a sense of commitment and responsibility that is shared by adults and students, and there is clear evidence of high expectations for both adults and students. The culture resonates throughout the building.

High-impact leaders monitor school climate and take appropriate steps to ensure that it is conducive to student learning. High-impact leaders understand that building respect takes active, intentional, and persistent effort. These leaders recognize that the transition from historical patterns of behaviors to new habits of practice and expectations doesn't take place overnight. However, they continue to provide opportunities for students to become active and responsible participants. Conditions are created that allow students to engage in the school community through exhibitions of their schoolwork on the walls and various in-school and out-of-school presentations.

In high-impact schools, teachers try to understand the unique characteristics of each student to find out what else is going on if there is a behavior conflict. Bound together by a sense of shared responsibility, high-impact schools work at building relationships with students, and teachers take the time to really connect with students. In this way, personal challenges and learning styles turn into special talents that can be the keys to a student's success.

In high-impact schools, teachers make sure that students who need extra time and extra instruction get it—before and after school, during lunch, and/or on the weekends. They assist struggling students and implement instructional programs to address the needs of all students. They may double up in a content area or get supplemental instruction to gain the extra time that is needed. These support classes provide help to students who enter underprepared. Students are provided the assistance they need to meet rigorous academic standards. They have multiple opportunities to succeed and can easily obtain extra help as needed.

In such schools, teachers and administrators maintain commitment to the focus, to the students, and to each other, despite challenges and day-to-day frustrations. These people willingly do whatever it takes to reach a vision for the school, to transport the school to a place where it has never been before. They feel they are being rewarded for their work in the success of their students. The culture is one of a community that fosters interactions and relationships based on mutual respect and trust. This gives them added leverage toward systemic improvement.

High expectations challenge educators as well as students. In high-impact schools, educators stretch beyond the level of support they have provided to students in the past. They recognize that in order for students to become more successful, higher expectations of the whole system are required.

It's About Perception

High-impact leaders make their schools the best they can be. The pivotal, imperative shift is from placing blame on students to accepting responsibility for accelerating the process for those who have fallen behind. Indeed, it is a challenge. But if this is not the responsibility of the school's leader, then whose responsibility is it? What are schools about? Why do they exist?

High-impact schools succeed with students who are usually on the wrong end of the achievement gap—poor students and students of color. Such schools are not common, but their very existence stands as proof that schools can do more than we have expected in the past. These schools serve as a powerful reminder that it really is possible to teach all children at high levels. It can be done.

High Impact Leadership: Improving Practice
Self-Assessment Tool

High Expectations for Every Student	Absent	Developing	Good	Exemplary
We share a belief that every student can learn, and we will do what is necessary for every student to achieve.				
We are committed to the study of best practice so that every student can achieve at high levels.				
We provide extra support to get students on track and keep them on track.				
We encourage every student to take on academic challenges.				
We ensure that all students are in rigorous learning environments.				
We have high expectations for all students regardless of students' prior academic performance.				
We use data as a warning system so that we can intervene early when students are struggling.				
We design interventions that address the *cause* of lower achievement.				
We recognize and honor excellence in achievement and behavior.				
We help our students develop a sense of responsibility and self-reliance.				
We take responsibility for every student to succeed.				
We put our students in a position where they can have choices.				

Next Steps ... REFLECTION and ACTION!

High Expectations for Each and Every Student

♦ What do I do each and every day to ensure there are high expectations for each and every student?

♦ Strengths? (Good and Exemplary Practices)

♦ Challenges? (Absent or Developing Practices)

♦ What actions will I take to better move our school forward to achieve high expectations for each and every student?

♦ What should we celebrate and how?

Chapter 3

Building Communities of Learners

Leadership and learning are indispensable to each other.
—John F. Kennedy

Strong learning-focused communities offer professional support and provide learning opportunities and mutual accountability for improving instruction. Principals must build a work culture that promotes collaboration, knowledge sharing, and collective responsibility for improving teaching and learning.

High-Impact Leaders Ask:

- ♦ When do teachers come together to talk about teaching and learning?
- ♦ What are the expectations for teachers to continue their professional development?
- ♦ Have we established a culture of questioning and inquiry?
- ♦ Is professional development site-specific and aligned with the needs assessment and goals of the school?
- ♦ Do teachers use assessment results to drive instructional decisions on an ongoing basis?
- ♦ Do teachers have opportunities for looking at student work?
- ♦ Do we see ourselves as a community of learners that can continuously improve through collaboration, assessment of results, and reflection?

Collaboration—The First Step to Better School Performance

High-impact leaders focus on the key goal of creating a learner-centered school (DuFour, 2002). Their strategy is to raise student performance by building leadership and instructional capacity. Collaborative learning communities expand opportunity and input from individuals, anchor the school culture, and change the structures and processes of the school in response to the changing needs within the school.

High-impact leaders support a community of collaboration where everyone works together for a new vision of education with real impact on students. They create innovative cultures, develop shared beliefs and values about teaching, and value informed professional insight. This requires the development of leadership capacity at all levels.

In high-impact schools there is an underlying belief that people affected by decisions should be involved in shaping those decisions. These schools have found ways to involve more people in decision making, and at the same time, to create structures that ensure coordination toward common goals and facilitate communication and sharing among all members of the school community.

In high-impact schools, there is a friendly, relaxed forum for discussing instructional methodologies and philosophies. Reflection on teaching practices is encouraged in an effort to help teachers grow both personally and as a team, department, or grade level of professional educators. In high-impact schools, collaboration and communication are seen as important processes for spreading a culture of instructional improvement.

In high-impact schools, collaborative learning communities promote supportive interaction and discussion about learning and create a climate of experimentation. This reduces the isolation of teachers, which is one of the most serious barriers to school improvement. Collaborative learning communities are based on the belief that people are good at different things and that staff members are better together than apart. The focus is on using individual and group strengths to meet the diverse needs of students.

Broad-based teacher participation encourages better decisions and strengthens individual and group ownership of the school, its activities, and its initiatives. Individuals understand how their actions affect others within and outside the school; collaboration draws on the expertise and practical experience of people closest to the work and helps leaders anticipate the complex implications of decisions. Such involvement often helps initiate and implement improvements that best meet the needs of the students.

The challenge however, is to get all at the table to give up individual ownership of whatever areas they represent. The idea is to remove barriers between these areas and instead to find common goals and build a collective vision. This requires that many more individuals develop the skills to work together in a collaborative setting to make important decisions. Just because a group of teachers are seated together around a table does not mean they know how to work together effectively. It takes explicit training to learn how to function and excel within the group. The skills of consensus building, problem solving, and information analysis are needed by everyone, not only by a select few.

Relationships and Culture

Collaboration practices change the culture of the school.

In high-impact schools, relationships are organized into a caring community of shared educational purpose. There is a climate of intellectual development. Principals in high-impact schools pay attention to the nature and quality of interactions between teachers and students. They ensure that teachers continuously concentrate their efforts on achieving high standards for both teaching and learning.

High-impact leaders build a culture of commitment, collegiality, mutual respect, and stability. There is a belief system that supports peer coaching, collaboration, trust, shared responsibility, and continuous learning by the adults in the school. This requires ongoing development of people's skills in making fact-based decisions, working with diverse groups, resolving conflicts, and using effective strategies to build consensus.

High-impact leaders move away from the idea of principal as "captain of the ship." They encourage increased participation from staff members in shared leadership, thereby increasing the quantity of leadership available in the school (Tirozzi, 2001). High-impact leaders focus on sharing to bring out people's power and creativity, while making sure that the school mission is achieved and that accountability is met. They create appropriate structures in which educational issues and school policy may be discussed. Such leaders encourage teacher leadership by sharing power over key decisions. As a result, teachers communicate openly, express their concerns freely, and influence school actions positively.

High-impact leaders model collegiality by joining in with teachers to work collaboratively to improve conditions in the school.

These leaders are accessible to staff. They are not office-bound, but are instead out and about on the campus. They reach out to others to encourage greater involvement. They nurture an instructional program and school culture conducive to learning and shared commitment.

High-impact schools are communities of teachers who learn through ongoing collaboration and practice. Teacher professionalism is supported and encouraged. The principal develops a continuous learning environment. Teachers work together, bouncing ideas off of each other, exchanging and sharing strategies. Teachers feel valued, and they grow in confidence. Collegiality is rewarded through release time, recognition, space, materials, or funds.

In high-impact schools, the emphasis on collaboration and collegiality encourages a willingness by teachers to try almost anything they think will enhance the learning of the school's students. They try out approaches they have learned about through reading and professional development. They take the risk to experiment to find what practice is useful for the students in their school. Members of the school staff take the time to reflect and take their values seriously. There is an enduring culture of growth, learning, and development.

High-impact leaders build a culture of questioning and inquiry. This requires that they possess a high level of facilitation skills in order to support team inquiry and collaborative problem solving. They help teachers hold deep discussions on practice, differences in approaches, and conceptions of learning. Continuous improvement requires information sharing, objective analysis, and the ability to ask and answer difficult questions. High-impact leaders respect the embedded knowledge existing within the school.

Sharing and spreading effective practices is a hallmark of high-impact schools. In these highly successful schools, teachers adopt a collaborative spirit. They are open to learning from one another, and they are willing to embrace risk. They open their doors and invite peers, coaches, and principals to engage in collaborative teaching and learning. They observe one another in the classroom and invite consultants or learning strategists to assist them in acquiring necessary knowledge or skills. Significant improvement in student learning results where educators work with coaches and each other to frequently adjust their teaching methods to best suit students' learning needs. High-impact educators recognize the value of working together for change and know it's safe to talk openly with one another and to rely on one another for consistency. Shared communication is predominantly positive, leading to productive energy and sustained cohesion.

The high-impact leader sets the agenda, creates the opportunities, and skillfully interacts to produce high-performing, outcome-oriented teachers. These leaders are committed to providing teachers with a climate that fosters their accomplishments of school goals. High-impact leaders give teachers necessary resources and support for their continued professional development, involve them in making decisions in which they are stakeholders in the outcomes, and provide them the academic freedom to use the most effective practices to teach the required curriculum. High-impact leaders create structures and processes that enable teachers to make maximum use of expertise, energy, and initiative. High-impact leaders develop a supportive work environment.

Trust is the glue that holds the high-impact school together and binds teachers to their goals. Teachers have high expectations of each other and trust that colleagues are working toward common ends. Trust creates a safe learning environment for trying out new ideas, and extends an invitation to all to stretch toward a hoped-for future. High-impact leaders create trust with lots of talk. They appeal to the heart for substantial effort toward a common focus. As a result, teacher learning is energized.

High-impact leaders create a caring, productive environment. They foster the development of a positive school learning climate conducive to teaching and learning. They establish positive expectations and standards, maintain high visibility, provide incentives for teachers and students, and promote professional development. They encourage increased quality, establish a norm of critical inquiry, and seek continuous improvement. These leaders ask, "How does inquiry into performance focus on what students and teachers are learning?" A comprehensive professional development program allows everyone to understand his or her roles in the school, to feel empowered, and to participate as a change agent.

Teamwork

High-impact leaders exhibit a sense of teamwork and shared responsibility in improving teaching and learning. They establish a collaborative approach to finding solutions when conflicts or complex issues arise. This requires a high degree of cooperation and involvement. Involvement leads to commitment. High-impact leaders involve everyone in designing the strategies by which to move forward. They create a strong team effort to improve.

Team learning and collaborative problem solving provide the most effective and efficient vehicles for realizing maximum benefit from the people within the school. Groups of people working together can be more productive than individuals working alone, but in order for teams to function successfully the organizational culture must be receptive and supportive. In order to create this culture, high-impact leaders provide opportunities for all staff members to serve in leadership roles in charting instructional improvement. They create a feeling of trust through cooperative working relationships among the staff in the school.

In high-impact schools, there is strong teamwork across all grades and with other staff members. Everybody is involved and connected to each other. Members of the school community willingly work together to address issues and to work on plans for improvement and growth. Everyone works together to improve student learning.

High-impact schools develop teacher efficacy, the belief that one can make a difference for teachers, by empowering individuals and groups with the authority and responsibility to make and carry out decisions. In many schools there is a central team that acts as a coordinating team for a variety of other working teams, such as grade level teams, department teams, content teams, budget teams, or special purpose team. In high-impact schools, teams are empowered to make real decisions. Although a team may seek the principal's advice, the team makes the decisions. The central team serves in an oversight role, ensuring that teams are focusing energies and resources on the school's central mission.

High-impact leaders believe that teams at the school should do their own problem solving, even though in some cases it might be easier for the principal to make a decision or to come up with an answer himself or herself. High-impact leaders are focused on creating a climate of trust for decision making. They are focused on empowering teachers.

In high-impact schools, teachers work together as a team to try different approaches in the classrooms. Dialogue is vigorous and stimulating as the level of engagement increases for teachers. As a result, learning outcomes are richer for students. New ideas emerge and spread through the school. Ideas develop a momentum of their own. They transform into a movement. As a result, teachers continuously learn and grow.

Continuous Focused Professional Education and Development

In high-impact schools, everyone is teaching and everyone is learning.

High-impact schools create environments of collaboration—communities of professional practice. However, many teachers have a reluctance to join an extended professional learning community. Professional development is often needed to help teachers work more effectively as a team. High-impact leaders provide necessary learning opportunities that are focused on collaborative problem solving and collective development. The National Staff Development Council (2001) maintains, "Some of the most important forms of professional learning and problem solving occur in group settings within schools." A school culture that invites deep and sustained professional learning will have a powerful impact on student achievement.

High-impact leaders make sure that the "people" element of the school reaches identified goals. These leaders ask, "What new instructional strategies do teachers need to use to increase students' understanding and skill? How is professional development linked to student learning in our school? What professional development experiences do teachers need to help improve students' achievement? How can teachers better share information about students' progress?" High-impact leaders provide opportunities for professional development to teachers to keep them vitally engaged in continuously making adjustments to support the learning and development of their students. The professional development is ongoing and includes follow-up and support. This emphasis on follow-up reinforces the importance of the professional development and motivates teachers to continue developing their skills.

In high-impact schools, the professional development is site-specific and aligned with the needs assessment and goals of the school. It is teacher-driven; teachers have an opportunity to plan, select, and engage in professional development that meets their individual needs. In high-impact schools, teachers identify what they need to learn and how they best can learn it. They participate in the planning for their learning. For example, teachers gather evidence of improvements in student learning to assess the impact of their own professional learning on their own students. They use teacher-made tests, assignments, portfolios, and other samples of student work to determine if the staff development is having the desired effects in their classrooms. This examination of student work motivates teachers to continue with the development of their professional skills as they see their students continue to improve as a result of the professional development activities.

High-impact schools make professional development an integral part of how they think and work. The school devotes resources to ensure that teachers have the time and opportunity to reflect on their classroom practice and to learn from one another. High-impact leaders create processes for professional development and staff interactions about teaching and learning. In order for teachers to exert organizational influence over curricular and other matters, they must have opportunities to articulate their views as a group. They need structures to bring them together, and the time and places to meet.

High-impact leaders design specific research-based organizational support for adult learning. They schedule and coordinate opportunities for teacher education and collaboration around curriculum and instruction. As a result, teachers learn how to work with each other to deepen their knowledge and improve their practice. They learn how to seek information and skills to strengthen and expand their capabilities. They collaborate in making decisions about rigorous curriculum and effective instructional methods. They discuss student work as a means of enhancing their own practice. Some possible support structures include mentoring and peer coaching, study groups, collaborative inquiry of student work, and action research.

In high-impact schools, teachers actively learn about and share with each other how each student's academic, emotional, and social needs are impacting their teaching and what strategies and interventions have been most successful. The focus of learning is on the development of new professional practice that addresses the needs of the school and enhances each person's capacity to effectively engage all students in academic learning.

High-impact leaders engage teachers in study groups to improve instruction, encouraging adults to mentor or coach one another to improve instruction. These leaders encourage others to share their ideas. Genuine dialogue occurs as teachers wrestle with teaching challenges. An educator will try out a new instructional strategy, program, or structure and then critically assess its fit to the goals and the culture of the schools. Teachers are willing to try out new initiatives.

In high-impact schools, teachers engage in extensive discussions about the school and efforts to improve it. They participate in purposeful planning around the school improvement academic goals. High-impact schools sustain active discussion and establish structures for interactions and input through committees, teams, and other methods. Powerful professional development is realized through collaborative dialogue about school improvement planning (Steel & Craig, 2006).

High-impact leaders ensure that faculty meetings are productive teacher-centered learning experiences. Meeting times become opportunities for staff members to share about their learning and their instructional practice. Professional development is key. High-impact schools prioritize meeting agendas to where the first item of business is always addressing the improvement of student achievement. For example, these principals ask, "How well are we serving each of our students? Are we adding value to their lives each and every day through our actions as a school? What are we doing for our students that help them learn more effectively? How can we better share our best practices?"

The high-impact school values and supports the systematic development of its teachers and sees teachers as valuable resources. High-impact leaders recognize the importance of fully developing and using the abilities of teachers fully. The high-impact school consciously invests in teachers and staff as leaders and learners through ongoing education, training, and opportunities for continuing development. Individuals are encouraged to take responsibility in crafting and following through on professional and personal growth plans aimed at acquiring, practicing, and using new skills and knowledge to better serve students. These leaders nourish a sense of responsibility and ownership in teachers so they understand how their role contributes to measurable success of the school and how they can become engaged as full participants in its improvement processes.

Using Data for Instructional Decisions

High-impact principals are strong instructional leaders. They have strong knowledge and understanding that student performance data drive what goes on at the school and in the classroom. They use detailed analyses of student performance measures to understand how well the school meets state standards. They use the results to fine-tune the curriculum, and they strengthen instruction to address any weaknesses. As a result, professional development increasingly is focused on the collection, reporting, and application of data.

In high-impact schools, teachers are provided with a standard base of tools and principles for standards-based instruction. This training builds the foundation for data-driven teaching and enables teachers to effectively differentiate their instruction based on the results of the data while working toward one set of benchmarks or standards. This ensures that over time, all teachers in the school have a common platform of professional development.

In high-impact schools there is a continuous cycle of inquiry that supports ongoing reflective use of data. Collaborative teaching and learning based on data gives teachers a purposeful focus to improve learning. Data-driven teaching becomes a group sport. Teachers, with the benefit of data, collaborate across classrooms, across grades, and across disciplines to accurately assess student progress, determine problem areas and develop strategies to take students to higher levels of achievement.

In high-impact schools, school staff members work together to discuss and analyze student performance data. They work together to develop a set of key questions that focus on student performance to guide their review of the data. The questions structure the inquiry and encourage teachers to stay focused on student learning and performance. For example, they ask, "Who is learning? What trends and patterns do we see? Are there gaps in learning? Are there gaps in instruction? What additional data could help us better understand what we are seeing?" This increases a schoolwide comfort level with data use and also serves as a potent strategy for building teacher data analysis skills. These collaborative activities contribute to a better understanding of how data can be used to inform school improvement strategies.

High-impact leaders build a culture of innovation, where everyone is involved in action research and constantly collects, analyzes, and interprets data for continuous improvement. These leaders find ways to bring information and skills to teachers as a way to build school capacity. They redirect resources as necessary and see that information and skills are used in ways that contribute to a climate of experimentation, increased energy, and flexibility.

In high-impact schools, a significant factor is the quality of instructional collaboration. Schools institute "structured lesson meetings," where teachers share lessons and discuss instructional strategies and materials that might enhance the lesson. There is no more private practice—teachers have to see what is going on in other classrooms so they can learn from one another.

In high-impact schools, data is drawn from multiple assessments and is used to inform every decision. Using formative assessment produces significant and substantial learning gains while reducing achievement gaps. When schools are truly focused on student learning as their primary mission, they regularly seek valid methods to assess the extent and depth of that learning. Frequent common assessments are an important means for checking the level of student learning. Teachers collaboratively develop the assessments as well as score the assessments. Then the group discusses the resulting achievement data and information. The assessments provide timely insights into their students' learning. They are used to improve teaching and learning rather than to evaluate students and schools. Accessible student achievement data allows teachers to analyze whether their original teaching approaches worked, and, if not, to brainstorm other approaches that might be more effective (McTighe & O'Connor, 2005).

High-impact schools monitor individual student progress in terms of standards and indicators. Conclusions from the data analysis allow teachers to intervene with unsuccessful students and to refine instruction. The focus on data impacts curriculum and instruction. One practical tool is an ongoing cumulative record of all assessments teachers use to demonstrate students' mastery of knowledge and skills. High-impact leaders review these notebooks regularly.

High-impact leaders assist teachers in enhancing the quality of their data gathering, analysis, and application of findings. They schedule time for teams to meet, plan, train, and conduct data mining and analysis. They provide teams with critical reports and queries that teachers need to inform decisions. Over time, teachers learn to focus their efforts on high-impact issues, to set up their actions and strategies, and to use measurement processes to track outcomes. In some cases, teachers write specific plans on how they will address any student weaknesses that emerge from the analysis of the data. These practices enable data to drive school decisions, gauge progress, and redirect instruction for continuous improvement.

In high-impact schools, all decisions are based on data drawn from various sources and focus relentlessly on attaining the goal of success for every student. High-impact schools are proactive, not reactive, in their efforts to ensure every student's success.

Collective Faculty Action

High-impact schools use data to drive collective action. Teachers use assessment results on an ongoing basis to drive instructional decisions. They regularly discuss assessment results at meetings, identify what is working and not working, and formulate needed changes across content areas. All teachers take ownership in everything that is assessed. Teachers agree to try out new practices—even those about which they personally have reservations—if these practices are likely to better serve their students. The guiding question is "What is best for the students?"

High-impact leaders create a culture for collective faculty action, where teachers exert influence over curricular and other matters and have opportunities to express their views as a group. Opportunities are provided for teachers to discuss critical issues and to make important decisions by consensus so there is broad support. Decisions are made at the point of action to the extent possible. Teacher capacity is increased by providing greater autonomy through involvement in decision making.

High-impact schools are driven by a bit of idealistic optimism, as they are willing to put forward all their knowledge and skills to make the school environment successful for every student. An attitude is infused throughout the school anticipating success. However, this requires support in terms of resources. High-impact schools are flexible and responsive, able to change in accordance with changing circumstances.

High-impact leaders establish conditions to support the rapid development and improvement that is expected. They make time for teachers to work collaboratively. Their work is centered on school improvement, and reflective dialogue is encouraged. High value is placed on shared decision making, teamwide efforts, peer coaching, and active sharing of resources, ideas, and responsibilities (Dyer, 2000).

High-impact schools are places in which both students and staff are continuously learning new skills and knowledge. Teachers use a solid base of professional knowledge and experience as well as information about their students' interests, needs, and skills to identify important issues for exploration. High-impact leaders make the most out of the experience and knowledge that exists within the school. They cultivate the energy and hard work of the teachers into expertise and wisdom that will enrich the school and benefit the students.

High-impact schools create a driving vision, and then do what is needed to implement and extend that vision. Schools look for new solutions, however demanding and complex they may be. They know answers will require hard work, commitment, and relentlessness. High-impact leaders take risks, try innovations, and have the patience to continually refine the new approach.

In high-impact schools, teachers create shared experiences and a common language. They develop ways of interacting that permit continual reflection on the achievement of their purpose. They facilitate mid-course corrections in organization practice to further the vision. Together, teachers build an evolving, positive collective school identity.

Examining Student Work

High-impact leaders build support structures for looking at student work. They direct teacher energies toward activities that relate to clear and shared expectations for student success. The focus on student work provides teachers with an opportunity to reflect on evidence of student learning and therefore evidence of effective teaching. Looking at student work also clarifies learning expectations and provides opportunities for teachers to engage in collegial discussions about desired outcomes.

Teachers become better at teaching by participating in work sessions where they collaboratively look at student work. Does the work reflect curricular standards? Are most students actually achieving the standards? What adjustments need to be made to our teaching? The focus on working together to probe the evidence generates a process for starting and sustaining dialogue about teaching and learning. As a result of this genuine collaboration, teachers gain a better understanding of what teachers and students actually learn. Looking closely at student work together can yield a greater understanding about how well the school is serving its students and about what strategies need to be implemented for reaching all students better. The discussions about assignments, the connection between the work and content standards, their expectations for student learning, and the use of rubrics all facilitate the improvement of teaching and student learning.

High-impact leaders use the process to gain new insights into the complex business of teaching and learning. The review of just one full day of work that is collected from a sample of students can unveil a comprehensive and rich picture of the quality of the work of the school. It provides a unique cross-sectional view of the evidence. Approaching the data through collective inquiry brings the entire school together for an honest and thoughtful discussion

Growth and Excellence is Not an Option

Leaders in high-impact schools exhibit a professional attitude involving consistent, knowledgeable, and insightful analysis of their own practices as teachers and administrators. They continually examine the work of the school for strengths and weaknesses, and they search for clues to guide further skills and understanding.

In the information economy, successful schools must be knowledge-based, value-added enterprises. In this environment, teachers and administrators are collaboratively involved in learning about the most effective instructional strategies and technologies. Collab-oration allows high-impact leaders to enhance the quality of thinking of those within the school without issuing edicts or direc-tions. High-impact leaders create learning opportunities that enable teachers to become leaders capable of anticipating and leading pro-ductive change.

High-impact leaders are clear about their intention to produce growth-oriented, skillful practitioners. They are cognizant that this process requires both support and challenge. They work to build relationships and rigor in their day-to-day formal and informal interactions with colleagues. They are able to support teachers in stepping beyond traditional approaches. They explicitly state expectations for cooperation among teachers. They are able to change long-running habits of practice and move the school from a group of independent contractors to a community of collaborative professionals.

In high-impact schools there is a collective will to pursue higher levels of professionalism. High-impact leaders cultivate a climate where teachers explore expansive ideas and stretch themselves in pursuit of becoming more effective on behalf of their students.

The Power of Community

A high-impact school is a community of practice in which learning, experimentation, and reflection are the norm. There is a sense of common purpose based in a collective understanding of the com-munity served by the school and the staff's capacity to work together toward this common purpose. Everyone works together to assure that diverse voices and beliefs are heard and that consensus truly results in what is good for the whole school and every student.

High-impact schools are professional learning communities engaged in assessing and improving instructional practice. These schools are equipped to meet the needs of individual students and to accelerate the pace of learning. They do this through a high level of communication about a variety of issues after establishing oppor-tunities for collaboration. These schools value the exploration and improvement of teaching. They recognize and support innovative efforts that contribute to creating a positive climate and culture in the school. Collaborative work forms the backbone for developing an aligned educational experience and expands a school's vision and boundaries by involving more people in essential processes related to student achievement and school improvement.

High-impact leaders are proactive. They build a supportive learning environment that is healthy and intellectually stimulating. They create an environment characterized by a high level of professional practice paired with a high level of student engagement in the construction of new knowledge. Students feel respected and connected, and they are engaged in learning. Instruction is personalized to increase student contact with teachers. Professional development supports collaboration and collegial accountability.

The high-impact school dedicates itself to developing everyone's potential talents, centering its attention on learning. It continuously seeks more effective ways to enhance student achievement through careful design and evaluation of programs, teaching, and learning environments. The school and staff both demonstrate an enthusiastic commitment to organizational and personal learning as the route to continuous improvement. Seeing itself as a community of learners that can continuously improve through collaboration, assessment of results, and reflection, the school designs practical means for gauging its students' and its own progress toward clearly identified goals.

High-impact leaders build common identity for the school based on shared experiences that resonate with deep meaning for those involved. These leaders recognize the importance of simple actions such as posting photographs of group events, creating phrases that express school identity, taking time for celebrations of successes, or providing opportunities for teachers to reflect on the progress of the school. These kinds of individual actions add up to a strong history of shared experiences that become the essence of the school.

Collaborative learning communities have the rich potential to be catalysts for reinventing schools (Fullan, 2003). The key to achieving such learning communities is to arrange the circumstances so that individualistic and creative teachers begin to own them and learn to appreciate the advantages of such a collaborative culture for themselves. This requires high-impact leaders who imagine future possibilities, examine shared beliefs, ask questions, collect, analyze, and interpret data, and engage the faculty in meaningful conversation about teaching and learning. The result is true collegiality, based on shared work and common goals. Team learning, productive thinking, and collaborative problem solving replace control mechanisms, top-down decision making, and enforcement of conformity.

High-impact leaders build the capacity and will of the school to deliver on the understood promise of a valuable education for every student. Everyone works together toward a common goal.

High Impact Leadership: Improving Practice
Self-Assessment Tool

Building Communities of Learners	Absent	Developing	Good	Exemplary
I engage teachers in school improvement planning and decision making.				
Teachers are engaged in collaborative inquiry.				
We use data on a regular basis. We scrutinize the evidence to completely understand how well students are performing.				
We use data to plan for curriculum and instructional activities.				
I set aside specific time for teachers to collaborate.				
We use multiple measures to evaluate student learning.				
We use data continuously, collaboratively, and effectively to improve teaching for learning.				
Teachers continuously collaborate to adjust instruction based on ongoing student performance.				
Professional development is aligned to school goals and teacher needs.				
I assist teachers to work as a team to analyze student achievement data to develop appropriate lessons, interventions, and plans for improvement.				
I establish teacher leadership opportunities.				

Next Steps ... REFLECTION and ACTION!

Building Communities of Learners

♦ What do I do each and every day to build a community of learners?

♦ Strengths? (Good and Exemplary Practices)

♦ Challenges? (Absent or Developing Practices)

♦ What actions will I take to better move our school forward as we become a community of learners?

♦ What should we celebrate and how?

Chapter 4

Teachers Are
the Silver Bullet

The people's capacity to achieve is determined by their leader's ability to empower.

—James Maxwell

eachers in every classroom must be competent, caring, and qualified. Individual teachers have a profound influence on student learning, and the strategies they use to guide classroom practice should maximize the possibility of enhancing student achievement. Principals must help teachers succeed through supervision practices and reflective dialogue.

High-Impact Leaders Ask:

- ♦ How do we ensure that every student has an outstanding teacher?
- ♦ Do supervision practices support teacher growth and development?
- ♦ Are teachers challenged to examine assumptions about their work and rethink how it can be performed?
- ♦ Do teachers consistently match materials, instructional approach, and assessments to the state standards?
- ♦ Do teachers use instruction that engages and motivates students?
- ♦ Have we created a climate of experimentation—an environment where teachers are willing to take risks, to try new things?
- ♦ What issues do teachers identify as necessary to address in order to serve student needs?
- ♦ Do we have supports in place for new and struggling teachers?
- ♦ Have we assigned our best teachers to the students who most need them?

Building Instructional Quality—
The Key to School Improvement

We know that the single most important factor for a successful school is having an excellent teacher in every classroom. Quality teaching has a considerably higher impact on student achievement than does every other school-based factor. There is a significant amount of research that has shown that having an above-average teacher versus an ineffective one can translate to more than a grade level difference in the progress of a student over a year's period. And, these teacher effects are cumulative and long lasting, with the impact so great that if a student has poor teachers 3 years in a row, the student will most likely never recover. However, on the other hand, a student with three above-average teachers in a row is positioned for success. Gaps in achievement between different groups of students are significantly reduced. Given this reality, the most important responsibility of a high-impact leader is to enable all teachers to become highly effective.

High-impact leaders recognize that instructional improvement is the heart of the work of the school. This is the single major daily function which all other efforts must aim to support. Everything in the school is about improving the learning opportunities for every student in every classroom. Teachers are in this business, for the most part, because they too want to succeed in this effort. High-impact leaders build on this desire by recognizing the value that everyone brings to the table. They expect great things from everyone and provide the support for success.

High-impact leaders ensure that the schools' vision and purpose guide the teaching and learning process. They have a vision of what they want students to achieve, and they encourage teachers to join in the efforts to make that vision a reality. They keep that vision in the forefront by supporting teachers' instructional efforts and by guiding the use of data to evaluate the progress of the school. High-impact leaders consistently communicate that student learning gains are a priority. Their guidance and oversight help improve the quality of the education that students receive.

High-impact leaders create a culture that is about continuous improvement and continuous learning. They build professionalism and commitment to achieving the mission. This increases teacher confidence and creates willingness for teachers to support and build on each other's strengths. It also results in higher quality solutions to instructional problems as the pool of ideas, methods, materials, and options for instruction is expanded.

These leaders attend to teachers' affective needs by building a sense of community. They create collaborative environments, leading teachers toward evaluating student work, leading study groups, developing and sustaining leadership teams, and providing specific feedback on unit planning. Teaching is not isolated. According to Schmoker (1999, p. 55), "People accomplish more together than in isolation; regular, collective dialogue about an agreed-upon focus sustains commitment and feeds purpose; effort thrives on concrete evidence of progress; and teachers learn best from other teachers."

In high-impact schools there are high expectations, and adults are accountable for coordinated and aligned curriculum and assessment, and quality classroom instruction. Instructional improvement begins with everyone in the school supporting student learning and being held accountable to do so (Shannon, 2003).

High-impact leaders are open to innovation, but they retain a firm grasp on what is known to be true about the effectiveness of various practices. They understand the diversity of students' needs and continuously expand their own knowledge about what practices work best. They hold themselves accountable for keeping their knowledge on the cutting edge.

High-impact leaders use student achievement as the filter for sorting what is really important to the school. They eliminate distractions and competing programs that may interfere with teaching the school's learning goals. They create the conditions in the school that allow teachers to do their jobs effectively. High-impact leaders see their role as serving the teachers—helping them teach well.

In high-impact schools, there is a strong culture and clear sense of purpose that defines the way they do business. There is a tight structure around the clear and explicit themes that represent the core of the school's belief system. At the same time, there is a great deal of freedom given to teachers as to how these essential core values are to be honored and realized. Teachers are given the autonomy to make decisions about how to practice their craft. They can pursue these ideals in ways that make sense to them.

High-impact leaders focus on teaching and learning. They work with teachers in areas specifically related to curriculum and instruction. High-impact leaders promote quality instruction, supervise and evaluate instruction, allocate and protect instructional time, coordinate the curriculum, promote standards-based lesson design, monitor student progress, and make data-driven decisions. Exemplary principals champion their schools' instructional purpose. They are master teachers with expert knowledge of teaching strategies, curriculum content, classroom management, and child development (Fenwick & Collins-Pierce, 2001, p. 28). High-impact leaders maintain a relentless focus on improving student learning by improving teacher practice. They know that ensuring effective professional learning is a key strategy for school improvement.

Instructional Supervision

Supervision of instruction is critical as high-impact leaders take action to improve the quality of instruction and learning in schools. It is the process that administrators conduct for and with teachers to plan for the improvement of instruction. High-impact leaders develop a common vision of good instruction and then help teachers achieve that vision through monitoring and supervising teaching practice. Implemented correctly, supervision is a key element in achieving school success.

In order to be effective, however, supervision of instruction involves a commitment on the part of the principal to not only observe classrooms, but also to have previsit and postvisit conversations, follow-up and feedback, goal setting, assistance to make changes, mentoring and coaching, opportunities for professional development, and guided reflection. High-impact leaders make supervision a priority. They commit time and energy to establish a comprehensive supervision process by which they can continually evaluate the impact of professional practice on student achievement.

In high-impact schools, the supervision process is ongoing, supported, and fully integrated into the culture and operation of the school. It is not seen as fragmented or as an external requirement. It is seen as fundamental to significant and long-term change in instructional improvement. Teachers need support for their professional growth and learning. In high-impact schools, the supervision process supports this improvement of professional practice.

In high-impact schools, the supervision process is a continuous cycle of planning conversations, observation visits, and feedback conversations. These leaders ask, "What are your expectations in this classroom? How do you know if your students are learning?" These occur regularly and are, for the most, part informal. The ongoing dialogue helps build a strong sense of trust and willingness for teachers to make the needed changes that will impact student learning,

To support the supervision process, high-impact leaders are highly visible. Being visible reinforces the principal's vested interest in what goes on daily in school. They become more aware of the daily challenges and constraints that teachers encounter. This heightened awareness results in more conversations and interactions regarding instructional matters. As principals talk with teachers about instructional concerns, the planning of an observation is often prompted. Conversations about teaching and learning are at the core of teacher growth and development.

Planning conversations set the stage for a specific collection of data related to a strategy or technique that a teacher wants to work on to improve. These conversations are often five to ten minutes long and are used to establish an agreement about what the teacher wants to accomplish and what evidence is needed to determine if the teaching was successful and if students did, indeed, learn. For example, a teacher might want to know how effective his/her questions are at getting students to engage at higher levels of thinking. The teacher might ask the principal to write down the questions used by the teacher during the lesson. Thus, the teacher and principal develop a focus for an observation that is driven by a teacher-identified need. These brief planning conversations can be done during "snack and chats," campus walks, or even bus duty. The key is to make these conversations a priority, not bound to an office or a desk. Informal discussions prior to observations reinforce supervision as a tool for teacher growth and development.

Observations are designed to help the teacher. In high-impact schools, the principal simply collects data regarding teacher behavior and student learning that was discussed in the planning conference. The data is collected using any number of different observation tools, such as teacher-student verbal interactions, teacher movement in the classroom, on-task behaviors of students, verbatim transcriptions of the teacher or the student, and/or frequency of specific teacher behaviors. High-impact leaders record the data in such a way that it is meaningful and relevant to the teacher. They record the objective facts and leave the analysis for the feedback conversation.

Observation data is the tool for instructional growth. Information gathered during the observation helps teachers see discrepancies between current and desired practices. Systematic observation of teachers helps the instructor feel that they are part of the larger enterprise. High-impact leaders build their schedules to support frequent and regular observations. They make sure that they know what instruction is going on and that the quality of the instruction meets the desired expectations. They focus on collecting data about student engagement. High-impact leaders clearly observe classrooms to support and encourage teachers, not to punish them.

High-impact leaders provide constructive, objective, and actionable feedback on teacher practice. This feedback helps the teacher to target the areas that need improvement and then to improve their instructional effectiveness; it also helps the teacher design professional learning opportunities that address the areas for improvement. This feedback is based on objective data that is collected during the classroom observation. The feedback works best when it is specifically related to an agreed-upon goal that was set during a planning conversation and when it encourages teachers to analyze their own behavior. For example, the principal might ask, "How did you feel the lesson went? Did students learn what you wanted them to learn? How do you know? What does the observation data tell you about your teaching effectiveness? What worked well? What is your plan to improve your effectiveness to ensure all students achieve the specific learning standards set for the lesson? How can I help you make the necessary changes?" Feedback conversations generate enthusiasm for teachers to reach beyond their current practice and performance as well as to help them become more self-monitoring and self-modifying.

The high-impact leader stimulates self-directed growth and improvement in teachers through this cycle of planning, observing, and analyzing. This cycle provides a common ground for discussing academic improvement. It encourages teachers to think of themselves as professionals, not employees as they become more self-analytical and reflective. It also enables the principal to know teachers' strengths and weaknesses and to provide opportunities for individual learning. These leaders ask themselves, "Who are our strong teachers? How can we use them to help us succeed as a school community that provides excellent teaching for all students?" They also ask, "Who are our new teachers? How can we support them so that they continuously grow and develop as committed educators?" And they ask, "Who are our weak and struggling teachers? How can we assist and coach them so they can have a more positive influence on our students' learning?"

High-impact leaders work in concert with teachers to review, modify, and adjust their instructional efforts. They are very much "hands on," with the majority of the day spent monitoring instruction in the classroom or having conversations about teaching practice. They are adept at managing by wandering around (MBWA), which is really the art and practice of listening and learning. It is the most important practice for building relationships and establishing trust for high-impact supervision. Effective instructional leadership begins with spending time—lots of it—with teachers, in and out of classrooms, engaged in conversation about teaching and learning (Hale & Rollins, 2006). For example, on any given day, the high-impact leader might teach a class, volunteer to be a teacher's aide for a class period, invite a teacher for lunch and informal discussion in the principal's office, or help a teacher grade papers after school. The ultimate objective is to improve the level and degree of productive thinking of the adults in the school.

High-impact leaders establish conditions within the school that allow and support rapid improvement in instructional efforts. Opportunities for innovation provide chances to research new solutions, to visit other classrooms and schools to see what works, to conduct action research within the classroom, and to discuss the results within the school's professional learning community. Success is found by high-impact leaders who intentionally establish the conditions that allow new instructional approaches, materials, and attitudes that focus instructional efforts on student performance over curricular coverage. They offer intensified and focused instructional leadership, encourage professional conversations among teachers supported by a professional learning community, and provide regularly scheduled and utilized opportunities for collaboration, with appropriate levels of accountability for the critical roles each plays in this mission.

Each year, high-impact leaders know that there will be at least several teachers who are teaching at the school for the first time. Whether these are beginning or experienced teachers, they come to the school without an understanding of its history, culture, academic standards, or the school's means of achieving them. The principal organizes a committee of experienced competent teachers at the school to provide the new teachers with support and mentoring throughout the year. Support is structured and focused on curriculum and instruction. They are given model lesson plans and given opportunities to observe master teachers. In addition, he or she frequently meets individually with new teachers, making a special effort to understand each teacher's strengths, limitations, and goals. In this way, the principal accelerates the teacher's integration with the school's culture and better understands how to use the teachers to advance the school's emphasis on student performance.

High-impact leaders focus more on the learning opportunities provided students and on the work students do and less on the teaching process and the work teachers do (Southern Regional Education Board, 2004). Supervision entails working collaboratively with teachers in planning, scheduling, and leading students in academic work. The skills of observing, evaluating, and directing are supplemented with the skills of listening, questioning, probing, and guiding.

In high-impact schools, the focus on instruction and improvement of student learning is seen as the purpose of supervision. Principals employ strategies that supervise planning, assessment, the learning environment, student work, and the act of learning. Supervision is the central role of the high-impact leader. Their daily work is organized around it.

The teachers in these schools know that students depend on them for good instruction, and so attention must be paid to what is taught and how. Good instruction is recognized, and weak instruction is identified for improvement. Teachers believe in the performance and development culture of the school. They recognize the significant benefits of a comprehensive system of observation and conferencing.

Reflection

High-impact leaders encourage meaningful reflection on teaching and learning. They help teachers develop a critical awareness about their own professional practices. They challenge their teachers to examine assumptions about their work and to rethink how it can be performed. High-impact leaders help teachers work through a process of inquiry to understand more clearly the impact of their thinking and their actions. Gathering and reflecting on the evidence about teaching behavior is key to successful individual development and continuous improvement.

High-impact leaders encourage teachers to help them maintain their effort toward improvement. For many teachers, finding new ways to do things is difficult and often painful. Therefore, immediate and sustained quality support is essential to helping teachers overcome the challenges they often face when trying to implement new strategies. High-impact leaders facilitate teachers' self-reflection and analysis about the nature and impact of their performance so they can gain a new level of insight into their actions and their efforts.

High-impact leaders engage their staff in professional discussion, drawing on best practice ideas and research to guide their thinking and actions. They encourage teachers to reflect on what they are trying to achieve with students and how they are doing it. They facilitate the development of a shared language for describing effective teaching practices.

High-impact leaders facilitate cooperative work among teachers in the interest of improving student learning. Teachers talk about practice. These conversations about teaching and learning are frequent, continuous, concrete, and precise. Teachers observe each other engaged in the practice of teaching. These observations serve as the basis for reflection and dialogue.

In high-impact schools, teachers reflect on their practice to think about what they are doing really well and what they need to work on to improve student achievement. They engage in regular conversations about the teaching process and ensure that instruction is focused on achievement. They are continuously learning new practices or fine-tuning best practices. They are perpetual students of teaching.

Coaching and Mentoring

High-impact leaders see mentoring and peer coaching as important ingredients for school improvement. They recognize the importance of intellectual honesty and mutual respect. They help struggling teachers. They collect data through observations, hold pressing conversations about the teaching, and provide assistance through coaching and peer support. They don't let struggling teachers fail.

To foster teamwork among teachers of the same grade and subject, high-impact schools use a collaborative coaching model, which involves teachers working in weekly study groups to observe model lessons presented by a specialist or peer and to set goals and expectations for the next week. Teachers who have trouble meeting specific goals can have a specialist or coach observe their lesson, give feedback, and offer support. In high-impact schools, teachers don't improve all by themselves, sitting in isolation someplace or listening to a lecture. They learn by doing their work and collaborating with other teachers. Coaching can be particularly effective in helping teachers to implement a new change in the classroom.

High-impact leaders give recognition to those who show initiative and who perform well. For example, a principal might mail a postcard home to a teacher who has made progress in achieving student learning goals in his classroom. These postcards become treasured reminders to teachers of how important and powerful their work is.

These leaders build on the strengths the school has. They continually provide feedback and encourage sharing. They support those who need help and provide whatever is required. They provide opportunities for teachers to collaborate and learn from one another, and they offer support and coaching as needed. They listen and make the teacher's concerns their most important priority.

In high-impact schools, mentoring programs are established. Such programs allow experienced and competent teachers to be partnered with less experienced or beginning teachers in order to promote professional conversation and to provide professional role models. Providing time for new teachers to collaborate with other highly effective teachers is a key ingredient in successful growth and development. High-impact leaders value teachers as individuals and sincerely want to see them succeed and grow; they provide specialized support throughout the year.

High-impact leaders model the behaviors they want to see in others—talking about teaching and learning, attending seminars, reading professional materials, and encouraging teachers to do the same. High-impact leaders stimulate the development of teacher leadership skills and support teacher research. Faculty meetings, drop-in visits, and even hallway encounters become venues for discussion of the value of ideas and strategies and the results of experimentation.

Aligned Curriculum

In high-impact schools, teaching is part of the larger collaborative effort, not an isolated activity where teachers decide independently what to teach and when to teach it. Instead, there are structures in place that support the alignment of the curriculum to state standards. Teachers work together to match the materials, instructional approach, and assessments to the state standards. This helps teachers to become intimately familiar with state standards. State standards are visibly present in every classroom in the form of posters that list the key learning objectives. These posters provide each teacher with a specific guide to what they must teach in their grade level to ensure that students will be ready for the next level. Lesson plans are standards-driven, not textbook or materials-driven. In high-impact schools, teachers revise and refine the curriculum to make sure they are teaching the right "what."

In high-impact schools, curriculum, instruction, and assessment are aligned with state standards (Lewis & Paik, 2001). High-impact leaders provide a coherent vision for what students should know and be able to do. The curriculum is nonrepetitive; it moves forward substantially as students progress through the grades. There is schoolwide instructional consistency within grades and curricular alignment from grade to grade. High-impact schools teach a curriculum grounded in rigorous, academic standards, relevant to the interests and concerns of students and based on how students learn best.

High-impact leaders support appropriate curriculum mapping and instructional improvement efforts. Teachers collectively engage in work by planning, developing, researching, and evaluating the curriculum. They align their curriculum with state standards, and they develop assessments, pacing guides, and professional development aligned with that curriculum. The curriculum is defined and communicated for student learning. This activity not only provides for a well-designed curriculum, but it builds collegiality around teaching and professional learning.

In high-impact schools, principals ensure that each student is prepared for the next grade level by reinforcing that what is taught is aligned with what is intended for students to learn. They set up vertical teams—teachers in the same subject from different grades—that meet regularly to make sure there are not gaps in the curriculum. If any gaps are identified, high-impact leaders supplement the curriculum with additional resources and materials. They work with vertical teams to reduce redundant content. They see that instruction is similar from classroom to classroom. Careful attention is given to designing curriculum content that is accessible and engaging.

Standards-Based Classrooms

In high-impact schools, state-standards are used to guide curriculum and instruction. Teachers know and understand the standards and indicators. Teachers use standards to define the information and skills that students are expected to learn. They teach content aligned with the standards and indicators, and they assess the indicators at the high level and with the rigor used in summative state assessments (Reeves, 2007).

High-impact leaders ensure that academic objectives for every subject at each grade level are stated clearly and understood universally. The curriculum is written to support the timely teaching of all key skills and concepts in the standards. State standards are visibly present in every classroom in the form of posters that list the key academic objectives for that year in each subject area. These posters provide each teacher with a constant roadmap of what they must teach in their grade to ensure that students are adequately prepared for the following grade.

In high-impact schools, teachers systematically check textbooks and supplemental materials against the standards prescribed for learning. They determine if the textbook matches with the essential learning targets and when they do not match, additional supplementary materials are obtained.

High-impact leaders believe that standards are important benchmarks that can help students advance along on a continuum of learning. Standards focus the teaching and learning process. Still, the force that drives the school is not the state test. The high-impact school is driven by clearly defined statements of what students should know and be able to do as a result of their education.

Classroom Practices

In high-impact schools, all teaching is aligned toward achieving the school vision and mission. Changing demographics and the rigors of preparing students for the twenty-first century require that we rethink what we teach, how we teach, and how we assess student performance.

In high-impact schools, teaching methods are used that ensure ambitious and equitable performance from all students. Teachers use inquiry and project-based learning to provide more personalized and individualized learning opportunities for their students. Projects that are tailored to individual learning styles and interests engage students on a deeper level. Such projects give students ownership of their work, which is more motivating and, therefore, more meaningful.

High-impact schools develop or adopt instructional strategies and materials in line with school design and performance goals. Teaching is adjusted to focus and improve instructional programs. Teachers use instruction that engages and motivates students. They use scenarios and examples that are realistic and respectful of students' interests. High-impact leaders help students develop high-level problem-solving skills and the ability to apply knowledge to new and different situations.

In these schools, teachers use a variety of instructional strategies to foster curiosity, exploration, and creativity. Teachers plan challenging activities that are clearly related to the concepts and skills being taught. In high-impact schools, teachers emphasize deep understanding of important concepts, development of essential skills, and the ability to apply what one has learned to real-world problems. Teachers provide students time to meet rigorous academic standards.

In high-impact schools, teachers support active learning through instruction that encourages students to make connections with the content. Activities provide opportunities for students to express learning in a variety of ways. They reinforce student reflection. In high-impact schools, teachers schedule time for students to work together, teach one another, and have conversations about their learning. There is extensive use of student conversation and classroom discussion.

In high-impact schools, teachers and students become actively engaged in developing meaningful activities and rubrics that surpass minimal standards. Students learn to access their own work through rubrics. Students then learn what they need to do to demonstrate mastery and understanding. Teachers create a variety of learning opportunities that are interesting and student centered, such as hands-on learning experiences, authentic projects, or community-linked activities. The enriched curriculum is more meaningful to students because it is more motivating and engaging.

In high-impact schools, teachers become specialized learning managers. They apply professional beliefs and talents in student-centered ways. They fit the content of the course to the strengths and weaknesses of each student. They use evidence-based best practices. They create classroom environments that effectively support children's learning.

Such schools are supportive school environments that are focused on continual improvement. In high-impact schools, teachers use student feedback to make instructional adjustments, to reteach as necessary, and to encourage student efforts. Teachers take corrective action as needed to help struggling students. Examples of these interventions include discussions of written or performed work, narrative commentary, student-teacher conferences, focus groups of students, regrouping, parent conferences, peer tutoring, and/or after-school labs to enhance skill development. Students are actively engaged learners who have strong relationships with teachers. This combination of relationship-building and instruction adaptation has a significant impact on student engagement.

In high-impact schools, assessments are aligned with learning targets and purposes. Teachers use a mix of assessment methods that allow students to demonstrate what they know and what they can do. Assessment results are used to focus and improve instructional programs. Teaching is adjusted as needed following frequent monitoring of student progress and needs. High-impact schools develop the capacity to deliver personalized instruction.

In high-impact schools, teachers assess student work at regular intervals. The assessment methods are coordinated into regular three- to six-week review cycles whereby teacher teams continuously collect and analyze data to determine how well students are mastering the content. These assessments provide immediate and ongoing feedback about the effectiveness of the instructional strategy. Any decision to adjust teaching methods is based on frequent monitoring of student progress and needs. The goal of the assessment practices is to enable staff members to intervene in a timely and a direct way to accelerate students' progress. Teachers develop plans for each student to address areas of need, and teacher teams meet weekly to discuss the impact of interventions to meet such needs (Williams et al., 2007).

In high-impact schools, teachers work at developing different approaches to help each student master the skills and knowledge behind the standard. High-impact schools recognize that remedial classes that offer low-level activities and minimal instruction are not the solution. A recent Education Trust (2003) study found that students in remedial classes tend to do poorly in all their courses. Yet similar students taking challenging language arts and math courses do better in all content areas. High-impact schools make sure that every student is in a classroom where high-level thinking is expected and taught.

In these schools, the principal and teachers at all grade levels meet weekly to discuss curriculum and instructional programs, student performance, and other issues. These weekly meetings not only provide teachers with the opportunity to identify success, but also help them understand where they may need to move additional support or make teaching adjustments in the classroom. Principals in these schools ask, "How are we making sure that students do not fall through the cracks? How are we diagnosing learning problems? How can we understand which programs are getting the results that we want? How do we know if we are achieving our standards? How are we enabling our students to learn?"

In high-impact schools, teachers use research-based knowledge to evaluate effective teaching and learning and to isolate ways by which students learn. Teachers recognize the value of classroom and state assessments; they understand what the assessments measure, and they determine how student work is evaluated. In high-impact schools, standards and rubrics are some of the tools used to help assess student performance and understanding. In addition, benchmarking tests tied to district and state standards provide immediate feedback on the progress of students with respect to learning state standards. This information informs intervention, which can better get at the root causes. Student learning is continuously monitored as part of a comprehensive assessment for learning system. Data is collected and is used to determine a student's strengths and weaknesses so that individual instruction can be provided where needed. Sophisticated monitoring of student learning can drive rapid improvement and advancement for students.

Schoolwide Support

High-impact leaders assess how well the school is performing according to multiple indicators. They ask critical and constructive questions, emphasize the systematic use of data, and encourage careful monitoring of both teaching and student progress. They structure time to evaluate and monitor student progress. They review assessment results from teacher-made tests, school benchmarking tests, teacher observation logs, lesson plans, grade-level meeting agendas, cross-grade-level meeting agendas, and standardized state tests. They also review and monitor the multiple year trend data on academic performance for each classroom using a comprehensive data management system. All data is reported in a user-friendly manner so teachers can readily adjust the curriculum and instructional program on an ongoing basis.

High-impact schools use data to develop sound, cohesive plans that build on the school's strengths while addressing and strengthening its weaknesses. A comprehensive data management system enables principals to respond quickly and positively to very specific situations. For example, if the analysis of the school's sixth grade math performance shows that the grade level as a whole is not making adequate progress, the school can change teaching assignments to bring stronger math instruction to that grade level. These schools organize themselves to match teacher strengths with student needs. Teachers are purposefully assigned in these schools so that all levels of students have access to the most qualified and experienced teachers.

Data is used to focus on ways to improve curriculum and instructional approaches and to determine what support needs to be provided to strengthen teachers' instructional skills. This support may include targeted staff development, grade-level changes in teaching assignments, lead teacher interventions, mentor teacher interventions, peer-to-peer coaching for teachers, team teaching, and a reallocation of the necessary resources.

In high-impact schools, leaders work to engage their colleagues. They gather evidence related to the instructional expectations to stimulate collaborative, professional conversations about teaching and learning. They create learning teams, study teams, data teams, research teams that work together designing instructional units, analyzing data, developing assessments, sharing strategies, and celebrating success. High-impact leaders direct staff efforts in designing targeted instructional approaches to meet the special and specific needs of students. They talk with teachers about what they are seeing when they examine student performance data. These conversations stimulate teachers to share effective practices and positive happenings in classrooms by teachers.

In high-impact schools, formalizing collaboration is a core element for school improvement work. Supporting collaborative activities within the school drives the dialogue and discussion that is necessary for long-term sustainability. Real collegiality among teachers improves their ability to hammer out some of the real issues that they face. They pursue these challenges by researching effective instructional methods through an ongoing review of professional literature. They work together in implementing these methods. Teachers work collaboratively and coordinate their work, including work across grade levels and curriculum areas. Teachers collect data on a regular basis, analyze the data, and then modify instructional methods and activities accordingly. High-impact leaders know that if teachers get together to talk about their teaching, then their teaching will have more of an impact.

High-impact leaders cultivate a climate of experimentation—an environment where teachers are willing to take risks, to try new things. They encourage teachers to use innovative and intriguing ideas in order to improve learning outcomes. They use data to convince teachers to stay the course.

High-impact schools engage in a continuous cycle of innovation, feedback, and redesign in curriculum, instruction, and assessment to meet its students' diverse and changing needs. Teachers individually and collaboratively engage in professional dialogue and curriculum development to create a comprehensively, deeply aligned system. They vigorously discuss the root causes of learning barriers, comparing teaching approaches that might be more effective in reaching students. Professional development that promotes sustained interaction is seen as the most effective means of changing instruction to improve student learning and to develop educator capacity.

High-impact schools have consistent, integrated, and aligned interventions. Rather than adopting entire externally developed programs, high-impact schools often select parts of externally developed programs and integrate them into a coherent, internally-developed approach that meets the school's needs. They keep their interventions simple, streamlined, and limited in number so they can keep their professional development focused on key big ideas. Teachers receive ongoing training to help them integrate the strategies in their lessons.

In high-impact schools, high-impact leaders take strong and effective action to improve student performance. Specific intervention plans are in place for every classroom. Every student is tested every year in core subjects in addition to periodic benchmarking tests for diagnostic purposes. If any student is having trouble meeting the academic objectives, a specific instructional intervention takes place. There is a strong emphasis on reading, and students who are weak in reading are placed in classes where there are more opportunities for reading. This serves as an educational safety net for every student in the school.

From Compliance to Commitment

High-impact leaders direct a learning community of teachers in the understanding, ownership, and application of their talents as individuals. Leaders focus on talent discovery and development. They choose collaboration over control.

In high-impact schools, teachers take on leadership responsibility not because of a bureaucratic mandate, but as part of a problem-solving process. They accept responsibility for the development of schoolwide values and systems for reinforcing those values. They recognize the value of collaboration to their instructional practices and work to provide richer opportunities for students and to come to a common understanding of whole-school team responsibility.

High-impact leaders encourage and support innovation and creativity over demanding conformity and compliance. Teachers are encouraged to try new ideas and materials, to collaborate and to extend their own learning.

Best Knowledge—Best Practice

High-impact leaders help teachers recognize that they are making a genuine impact on the life of a child—an impact that is successful, worthwhile, reachable, and within reason. They focus on the positive—they focus on what people can do and are doing. They acknowledge what is working, what's changing, and what is improving. High-impact leaders hold the conviction that all teachers can make a contribution to student learning.

High-impact leaders understand that their basic work is to ensure improved teaching and increased student achievement. They do this by providing focus and direction to curriculum and teaching, establishing conditions that help students achieve, and inspiring them to reach for ambitious goals. High-impact leaders ensure that every thoughtful change made at the school helps it move closer to its vision of all students becoming successful. High-impact leaders take on the role of being a "teacher of teachers" (Beck & Murphy, 1993).

High-impact leaders are significant factors in facilitating, improving, and promoting the academic progress of students. They know that better teaching leads to improved student achievement; therefore, they guide, encourage, reinforce, and promote teachers' instructional efforts. High-impact leaders make a deliberate effort to communicate directly and frequently with teachers about instruction and student needs.

Such leaders are a visible presence in the classroom. They use evaluation of teacher practice to inform school improvement efforts. They solicit and provide feedback on instructional practices, creating a climate of collaboration. As a result, teachers are willing to request the principal's help in improvement of their teaching.

High-impact leaders consistently use the school's core mission as the framework within which to design professional development, to pilot programs, and to implement new initiatives. Professional development is evaluated in relation to its impact on student learning and improvement of teaching practice. In high-impact schools, quality teaching and learning are supported by ongoing professional development that is job-related and focused on the learning needs of students. Ongoing professional development is coupled with close attention to classroom practice and coaching for teachers when necessary. Learning opportunities are provided so teachers can develop the skills and knowledge necessary to teach to higher professional standards. In high-impact schools, knowledge and skill serve as the foundation of support when leaders enter into new educational frontiers.

In high-impact schools there is extensive use of student assessment data by the principal in an effort to improve instruction and student learning. For example, high-impact leaders use standards-aligned assessment data from multiple sources to evaluate teachers' practices, to identify teachers who need instructional improvement, to identify struggling students, and to develop plans for interventions.

High-impact leaders provide teachers with formats, structures, and plans for reflecting on, changing, and assessing their practices. They encourage teachers in self-evaluation and goal setting for improvement. They assist teachers to be self-directed and self-managing.

High-impact leaders learn about curriculum in order to discharge their responsibility effectively in implementing standards and accountability. They have a solid understanding of student assessment and continually look for ways to show that kids are learning. They stay abreast of best professional practices and help create conditions for professional growth. High-impact leaders see themselves as on-the-job learners.

These leaders know how to capitalize on the strengths and interests of the teachers in order to stay the course of improving the school. They build on people's present skills to engage them and motivate them to continue to grow and develop. They find the balance between trusting that everyone is going to do the job and needing to intervene.

High-impact leaders stress standards for professional performance by teachers. The entire school community is on the same page with regard to what is being taught, what the performance expectations are, and where each teacher's curricular focus fits into the broader curriculum of the school. A constant focus on teaching and learning is basic to the culture of the school.

In high-impact schools, the teacher's work focuses on enabling students to understand the expected learning standards and to achieve what is laid out in them. The high-impact leader's work is to enable teachers to be successful in accomplishing that.

High-impact leaders continually look at the way they structure, observe, and improve individual teaching. They develop processes to provide what every student deserves: teachers in every class-room who are the greatest learners of their own practice and who offer an intellectually challenging, relevant education.

High Impact Leadership: Improving Practice
Self-Assessment Tool

Teachers are the Silver Bullet	*Absent*	*Developing*	*Good*	*Exemplary*
I visit classrooms on a regular basis to assess the quality of education that our students are receiving.				
I focus on student learning results to inform curriculum, instruction, and assessment.				
I model, coach, and facilitate best practices of teaching for learning.				
I provide opportunities for teachers to explore new strategies for better meeting the needs of students.				
We ensure that the curriculum taught is aligned with state standards.				
I provide opportunities within the school for teachers to learn continuously.				
I regularly conduct planning meetings before observations.				
I regularly conduct feedback meetings after observations.				
I collect specific objective data during classroom observations.				
I encourage reflective practice.				
I provide one-on-one guidance and assistance to teachers enabling them to continuously improve their instruction and student learning.				
I challenge ineffective teaching.				

Next Steps ... REFLECTION and ACTION!

Teachers are the Silver Bullet

- What do I do each and every day to support teacher growth and development?

- Strengths? (Good and Exemplary Practices)

- Challenges? (Absent or Developing Practices)

- What actions will I take to better move our school forward to ensure that every student has a competent, caring, and qualified teacher?

- What should we celebrate and how?

Chapter 5

Creating a Coherent System for Continuous Improvement

Success on any major scale requires you to accept responsibility.... In the final analysis, the one quality that all successful people have is the ability to take on responsibility.

—Michael Korda

rganizational processes and practices are critical to the development of a coherent system of support for the improvement of teaching and learning. School effectiveness and the level of impact on student learning depend on the alignment of resources, structures, time, and decisions with each other and with a focused improvement agenda.

High-Impact Leaders Ask:

♦ Are our strategies, structures, practices, and processes aligned to our mission and our vision?

♦ Do we maximize our use of time?

♦ What do we need to make this idea work? How can we make this happen? What can we do with what we have?

♦ Have we built our organizational capacity to support our improvement work?

♦ What types of structural changes might make a difference for our students? Why?

♦ Have we engaged our school community to support our efforts?

♦ Do we need to adjust the way we do business?

School Processes and Practices

High-impact schools engage in practices and processes that support the ongoing improvement of teaching and learning. Their student-focused processes support continuous improvement, open communication, and flexibility. The emphasis on academic success influences the selection of instructional materials, instructional strategies, use of fiscal resources, scheduling the school calendar, assignment and use of people, and use of classroom and building space.

High-impact schools evaluate the quality of school processes in order to provide explanatory information when student output goals are not reached. These schools examine internal conditions to determine what needs to be changed in order to improve teaching and learning. Understanding school processes and practices may point to possible causes and thus to possible solutions for inadequacies in school outputs.

The high-impact leader constantly engages teachers in conversations about changes in processes and practices the school needs to make to enhance student performance. High-impact leaders continually review the day-to-day operations of the school in order to better understand the organizational effectiveness. They begin no new program or launch any new initiative without examining the impact the initiative might have on current system practices and the relationship it will have on improving instructional quality.

High-impact leaders focus on people and processes rather than on paperwork and administrative minutia. Time is spent on value-added activities that lead to better system capacity. High-impact leaders engage in continuous reflection to identify and develop processes and systems to improve student learning and to strengthen instructional and organizational effectiveness.

A study by Heck and Marcoulides (1993) found that: (1) effective and ineffective principals differ in how they allocate their time as well as in the quality of their instructional leadership actions, (2) high-achieving schools involve teachers in critical decisions about instruction, (3) principals who are instructional leaders pay attention to setting goals and allocating resources to align with such school goals, (4) principals who are instructional leaders use student performance data and monitor student progress (pp. 26-27).

Mindful that education serves society, the high-impact leader continually examines school practices to make certain their effects and results actively contribute to the common good.

Strategic Alignment

High-impact schools provide an aligned instructional system to support student learning. They focus first and foremost on establishing a strong foundation of excellent, coherent schoolwide practices related to the core standard-based curriculum, on assessing and monitoring student academic achievement, and on providing the adequate support teachers need. Decisions are based on students' need rather than on the adults' need, and all processes and systems are structured by and aligned to what provides the most support to increase student learning.

High-impact schools focus on defining and implementing processes that can support instructional effectiveness. They redesign the way the school operates to streamline processes and to create consistency and constancy. They continually examine the alignment of structures, processes, and practices to the school's vision.

High-impact leaders develop a clear description of their schools' strengths and limitations to identify areas in need of improvement and to develop strategies that can be implemented to facilitate improvement. They provide strong implementation support. This assistance ensures that implementation efforts are successful. By making sure that necessary resources, structures, and policies are congruent with each other and the efforts, all energies focus on accomplishing the mission. High-impact leaders engage at every level to align development efforts with long-range school improvement plans.

High-impact leaders see patterns and relationships, and they appreciate that all actions within the school are connected. They understand and acknowledge the interconnectedness of school practices. High-impact leaders understand that while each practice stands alone, the way all practices relate, interact, or reinforce each other is equally important.

Organizational Structure

High-impact leaders develop and modify the organizational structure to achieve the school's vision and to establish positive conditions for teaching and learning. They are able to create structures and processes that bring the core values and principles to life, and then they are able to translate them into action. They get rid of obstacles to change or processes that seriously undermine the vision. They encourage risk taking and nontraditional ideas, activities, and actions. They also make tough decisions to remove people who do not ascribe to the vision.

High-quality instruction serves as the fundamental principle that guides school practices. Often, instruction is viewed solely as the concern of classroom teachers. In high-impact schools, school processes and structures support quality instruction.

High-impact schools make necessary structural changes in order to catalyze reforms in how the school functions and to open up new ways to align resources of the school (that is, the available staff, time, and space). Structural changes in high-impact schools create new opportunities for using time, organizing groups of students, spending funds, and deploying adult resources (Kannapel & Clements, 2005).

High-impact schools clearly communicate the connections between organizational structures and instructional practice. They understand that the reason for making structural changes is for improvement of student outcomes. Teachers are given an opportunity to suggest and shape structural changes, try them out, evaluate the results, and then adapt practice to improve outcomes.

High-impact leaders recognize that the pacing of organizational changes allows for variation in implementation. In other words, it may not be reasonable to expect a newly implemented schedule to work thoroughly and completely in just 1 year.

In high-impact schools, structures that encourage engagement in the tasks of the school as a whole enable teachers to develop confidence in each other. In these schools, leaders are actively engaged in creating safe and orderly learning environments, providing opportunities for meaningful student involvement, and developing collaboration and cohesion among teachers. The structures are organized for students and staff success in achieving the schools' goals.

High-impact leaders identify the organizational changes and support systems necessary to implement the school's mission and vision. These leaders strive to make sure their organizational structures (e.g., accountability systems, community engagement, and the use of resources such as time and money) support school goals. High-impact leaders articulate the connections of the new practices and structures to school success. They use reliable, participative, and practical methods for school improvement and organizational growth.

High-impact leaders establish organizational structures that expand the capacity of the school to realize its vision and reach its goals. They develop a supportive work environment by establishing important organizational structures and processes that support the teaching-learning process. High-impact leaders focus on planning and developing intentional group collaboration. They create opportunities for informal groups that lead to a sense of community and a shared responsibility for learning and adaptation. Structures are in place to promote collective activity for teachers to develop and implement programs. These structures facilitate organizational change.

Coherent Management

High-impact leaders focus on the coherent management of school operations to support student learning. They unravel bureaucracy and put supports in place to alleviate uncertainty. These leaders create conditions for success through effective organizational and management practices that support learning and instructional performances effectively, create clarity and trust, organize staff time effectively, and are strong on implementation, operations, and project management. High-impact leaders provide the organizational oversight and the know-how to enable teachers to carry out the school's mission competently.

High-impact leaders engage in a systematic analysis of instructional and organizational effectiveness in order to make informed management decisions. These leaders examine operational procedures to maximize opportunities for successful student performance. They employ a comprehensive and thorough data collection system to search for deeper understanding of the quality of the processes in the school on behalf of student learning.

High-impact leaders create the conditions for effective use of student performance data throughout the school to determine school impact. They do this by sharing leadership responsibilities and by creating symbiotic organizational structures such as data teams and data coaches. This fosters a school culture that embraces the use of data to make instructional decisions. Data coaches model the productive use of data; thereby encouraging the staff to develop a deeper understanding of the useful role of data in school improvement. High-impact leaders facilitate effective organizational management through the regular use of information and data to inform decision making. They accept responsibility for school management and operations, and they follow through on implementing needed changes.

Time

In high-impact schools, time is viewed as a resource for supporting student learning and enhancing the productivity of the school. The belief that student learning matters most leads to the investment of time and resources to help students grow to their unique potential.

High-impact leaders manage time to maximize attainment of organizational goals. They use time as a resource to more effectively serve students. They are emphatic about protecting time for instruction. For example, they limit interruptions to instruction by prohibiting students from being pulled from class except for emergencies and ensuring that PA announcements do not occur during class time except under extreme circumstances. They see time as a precious commodity to be guarded. They are willingly receptive to any change that will produce more time for students to learn and more time for teachers to improve their skills, to plan, to reflect, and to assess students' performance as well as their own. High-impact leaders develop policies and operational procedures that protect instructional time and promote increased allocations of instructional time. "The [principal's] quest is to find and create organizational structures, teaching environments, and working conditions that encourage teachers to become researchers of their practice and reflective practitioners (Smith, 2001).

In high-impact schools, organizational processes, teacher responsibility, and structures of time and space are reviewed and adjusted to support collaboration. Opportunities are created for teachers to learn together through study groups or other similar structures; efforts are made to find time for professional work during the school day to the extent possible. Specific changes to school organization could include: using common planning times for teachers, assigning teams of teachers to groups of students, setting aside regularly scheduled blocks of time for in-depth professional development, developing teacher work groups for given projects, or implementing professional development that promotes collaboration such as faculty study groups.

High-impact leaders know there are no shortcuts to learning—not entertainment to instill motivation, not lower standards to create opportunities for "success." Instruction, practice, feedback, correction, and more practice are the critical steps of formal learning experiences. Facilitating learning is hard work, and high-impact leaders know that much time and effort are required for low-performing students to meet high standards. Every aspect of the school's structure or operations or schedule must focus on teaching and learning, and providing more time for both.

Resources

High-impact schools understand that a passion for learning is only the foundation of a solid education. Students and teachers need and should expect the right tools to help them achieve academic excellence. High-impact schools offer more of the right learning tools to their students than do average-impact schools. High-impact schools focus time, energy, and resources on helping every student achieve. These leaders ask, "How can we connect improvement activities, resources, and learning agendas?" In high-impact schools, resources are fully dedicated to achieving the goals of the school.

High-impact leaders align every resource in the school in the service of instruction. They place students in the center of attention and find the resources to support this vision. High-impact leaders are strategic in their use of school resources, allocating new or supplementary resources to promote student learning in a coherent and unified fashion. These leaders have the skills and confidence to act as wise consumers and managers of resources, and they pay close attention to the ways existing resources are deployed to maximize effectiveness for students.

High-impact leaders manage resources responsibly, efficiently, and effectively. They ensure that the human, instructional, financial, and physical resources are allocated in alignment with the schools' missions and goals and that these resources are used in ways that advance productive student learning. High-impact leaders have an in-depth knowledge of the resources available to solve problems. They also have quick, perceptive decisiveness in applying that knowledge, and as a result, they may recast existing resources in the service of advancing the schools' improvement initiatives.

High-impact schools allocate resources strategically. They continually review and reallocate the resources necessary to support quality instruction. They realize that because not all students learn at the same rate, additional resources might be needed to support low-performing students. High-impact leaders are able to find necessary materials and strategies to accelerate the pace of their struggling students.

In high-impact schools, everyone works together to analyze the relative strengths and weaknesses of school operations, and focuses on strategic allocation of resources to promote desired outcomes. High-impact leaders plan for, articulate the requirements of, and compete effectively for resources to meet school needs. High-impact leaders provide opportunities through which the school staff can make choices about the use of the resources at their disposal to support the larger purpose of the school.

High-impact leaders view themselves as being "resource people." They recognize the importance of nurturing their teachers by providing them with enough up-to-date instructional materials for all students. They provide equipment and opportunities students need to learn and to be successful. High-impact leaders stay informed about what is going on in classrooms, and as a result, they are able and willing to provide needed support for teachers to achieve the desired student outcomes. They provide a supportive workplace that includes the curricular infrastructure within which teachers can work effectively.

High-impact schools devote resources to content-rich professional development, which is connected to reaching and sustaining the school vision. High-impact leaders align professional development to organizational goals. They ensure that professional development opportunities are continuous over time, research-based, culturally relevant, and connected to personal professional practice. These leaders provide the necessary support for the meaningful implementation of the curriculum.

High-impact schools carefully coordinate the school improvement plan and the budget. Budget allocations and expenditures demonstrate a direct link to academic objectives. High-impact schools make a continual commitment to using student data for outlining these expenditures.

High-impact leaders orchestrate resources and manage distractions so that staff members do not become overwhelmed with the numerous interferences that often plague schools. High-impact leaders know how to take advantage of resources and how to create organizational arrangements that nurture competence and support new initiatives. These leaders are always thinking about ways to get more from resources at their disposal, including staff time, materials, space, and budgets. They are continuously creative in thinking about ways to reorganize and do things differently with the goal of better meeting the needs of the students.

Parent-Community Engagement

High-impact leaders are actively engaged in securing outside support for school goals and forging links between the school and the larger community. They fine-tune community interactions with the school and remove barriers to communication. They maintain high visibility with the larger school community. They identify and nurture relationships with community members. High-impact leaders establish partnerships with parents and community members to strengthen programs and support school goals.

High-impact schools engage parents and community members as partners in the learning process. They recognize the important interconnected role that families, communities, and schools play in helping all children succeed in school and in life. High-impact leaders recognize the important strengths, skills, perspectives, and knowledge the community brings to the educational processes. High-impact schools welcome and respect these contributions.

These schools encourage varied and imaginative forms of communication between school and homes. They provide many opportunities for parents and community members to be involved in governance and decision making. High-impact leaders promote collaboration with the community.

High-impact leaders build collaborative networks of support for the work of the school. They continually examine the way they communicate with constituents, gather and use data, and get feedback. They create processes that foster two-way communication rather than channels that direct the flow of information in only one direction. They foster productive and meaningful opportunities for parents and community members to offer substantive contributions to advance the school's mission.

Policy

High-impact leaders align policies, operational procedures, and the allocation and use of resources with the educational agenda of the school. The school's core values, beliefs, and mission serve as the decision filter for the development of schoolwide policies and operational procedures. They translate high expectations for student learning into policies and practices (Knapp, 1993). They review and revise policies, as needed in order to closely link programs and practices to learning goals. Successful schools need ongoing, sound, effective, and flexible policies and practices to ensure consistent achievement gains. High-impact leaders ensure that policies are consistent with their school's vision and goals.

Building Capacity

High-impact schools continually monitor their performance and develop the capacity to manage their own self-improvement. They engage in value-added assessments aimed at organizational growth. They use a flexible accountability framework to support the dispersion of effective practice across the school. These practices help high-impact schools become more responsive to immediate and future needs in terms of planning and achievement.

High-impact leaders recognize that practices, procedures, decisions, resources, policies, and direct encouragement make it possible to make and sustain the changes implied in a school's purpose and vision. This support reflects the leaders' true commitment to attaining the school's vision.

Making a Commitment

In high-impact schools, there is a culture of continuous improvement and learning. There is a system of collaborative approaches designed to support the implementation of research-based strategies that encourage improvement. High-impact schools maintain a constant and steady focus on improving student learning through the continuous improvement of instructional practices and organizational conditions.

High-impact leaders establish supportive environment conditions for rapid development. They see change as an opportunity for positive growth and improvement and so they create the conditions that support productive change. They sustain the commitment to continuous improvement and renewal. They are able to tackle the challenges that naturally come with leading change.

High-impact leaders motivate all teachers to be advocates for continuous improvement. They consistently ensure that school improvement planning focuses on improving student learning and instructional effectiveness, rather than on school structure, policies, and regulation.

High-impact leaders provide skillful stewardship for continuous improvement by ensuring effective management of the organization, operation, and resources of the school. They champion careful design and rigorous evaluation to prevent problems before they occur and to enable the school to systematically strengthen its programs, pedagogy, personnel, and organizational practices.

Leaders like these become facilitators, coaches, servants, and strategic mentors as they lead their schools to greater success. They understand the difference between leadership and management, and they find time for both. High-impact leaders achieve an extraordinary balance between task orientation and people orientation. This makes a significant difference in student achievement.

Schools change over time. In high-impact schools, people can articulate the changes they are consciously trying to make and can identify where they are in the process. Members understand that their school does not arrive at its final destination instantly, but instead develops one step at a time. High-impact school members have a clear sense of what they're trying to do, what progress they have made, and what still needs to be done.

In high-impact schools, distributed leadership and collaborative development of the school are seen as the keys to ownership and that pride of ownership is what drives continuous improvement of the school. High-impact leaders use decentralized decision making to involve more individuals in making and implementing decisions critical to school improvement. These leaders conduct dialogue sessions to identify the perceived strengths and limitations of the work of the school. High-impact leaders provide sufficient time during which teachers can collaborate and reflect on the school's goals and school improvement initiatives. The school's organizational system and culture stress the importance of continuous improvement.

High-impact leaders focus on changing the culture from teacher-centered to student-centered. In student-centered schools, the teachers take responsibility for student learning—they recognize that they are the ticket to students' success. Extraordinary efforts are made by the school to honor the outstanding work of students and staff.

High-impact schools connect the spirit of caring with the practical business of learning. They move from strategy as a fixed plan to a learning process that leads to continuous improvement and develops the school's ability to cope with changes in their environment.

High-impact leaders do not exercise control through hierarchical authority, but instead forge consensus and mobilize talents to enhance student performance. These leaders ask questions and suggest a variety of alternatives that expand conceptions of how organizational tasks should be accomplished rather than telling teachers how these tasks might be accomplished.

High-impact leaders remove impediments to progress. They make sure that everything they do is focused on the improvement of achievement and equity.

A school thrives when its leadership actively creates and supports a quality-driven culture. It becomes successful when the principal models values and behaviors that communicate a comprehensive and focused vision to all constituents. Leaders have a responsibility to make sure that everyone understands and values the school's mission, goals, and directions—and uses this understanding to inform their individual work goals and decision-making strategies.

Such leaders work to help students and other stakeholders share this understanding as well. They ensure that the school's systems and processes align with its mission and vision, making certain that the necessary resources—people, funds, facilities, equipment, supplies, time, energy, and other assets—are allocated and used in support of the overall mission and vision.

High Impact Leadership: Improving Practice
Self-Assessment Tool

Creating a Coherent System for Continuous Improvement	Absent	Developing	Good	Exemplary
We use data to measure the effectiveness of the school and its processes.				
We continually examine the organizational and structural changes that might make a difference for our school.				
I involve teachers in determining resource needs and allocations.				
I have allocated time to support teaching for learning goals.				
We have put instructional structures in place to support professional learning opportunities.				
We have put instructional structures in place that facilitate teachers' work in learning teams.				
We have realigned the use of resources to better serve our students.				
I have deployed human resources to maximize student learning.				
Our budget is aligned with school improvement goals.				
I create opportunities for parents/ community to learn about and get involved in curricular and instructional activities in school.				
I spend the majority of my time as an instructional leader as compared to a school manager.				

Next Steps ... REFLECTION and ACTION!

Creating a System for Continuous Improvement

♦ What do I do each and every day to ensure our strategies, practices, and processes are aligned to our mission and vision?

♦ Strengths? (Good and Exemplary Practices)

♦ Challenges? (Absent or Developing Practices)

♦ What actions will I take to better move our school forward to ensure that our practices and processes support ongoing improvement of teaching and learning?

♦ What should we celebrate and how?

Conclusion

High-impact leaders know that improving schools is challenging and that change that drives improvement in schools requires honesty, persistence, and a good deal of knowledge about school systems, learning, and leadership. However, high-impact leaders also know that change can take place and that it is not as hard as it seems at times. High-impact leaders recognize that the capacity to create high-impact schools already exists in their schools. They know that by creating a community where there is a shared commitment to serving every student, meaningful change can occur.

High-impact leaders don't change schools by themselves—they use a wide-angle lens to keep the whole vision in view for the entire school. They have the capacity to inspire in others the sense of commitment and passion it will take to make the necessary changes for the vision over the long haul.

High-impact schools deliberately foster a school community that serves as an advocate for equity, diversity, fairness, inclusiveness, and justice. These schools provide access to significant adults who help students feel collectively and individually valued. High-impact leaders help students develop the skills necessary for self-management, self-motivation, self-reflection, and self-direction. They prepare students to make significant contributions to the greater good. High-impact schools make responsible decisions that embrace standards of the heart.

In high-impact schools, vision anchors all decisions. High-impact leaders have the courage, patience, trust, and openness to keep the school vision vital and responsive. High-impact leaders act deliberately, with positive, enthusiastic attitudes. While keeping people focused on the vision, high-impact leaders affirm progress and celebrate success.

High-impact leaders have a mindset that improvement never stops; they continue to seek new opportunities for growth and development. High-impact leaders know that change takes time and implementation may take place in baby steps as they begin breaking new ground.

There is no magic solution, no single program, strategy, or theory that holds all the answers. Instead, solutions must be developed locally, by a process that meets the unique needs of each school's students. The quality of the transformation depends on the strength of the commitment.

The areas of action that have been presented describe an orderly sequence of activities and processes that yield reliable results. The principles and methods on which the book is based are formed from over 30 years of research. The ideas and practices are offered to help the leader and the school choose the best path for their unique students and teachers.

We have the power to change things—but the key to that power is the belief that it exists. This is the core to success in high-impact schools.

PRESS ON. The starting point of all achievement is desire.
—Napoleon Hill

HIGH-IMPACT LEADERS •
HIGH-IMPACT SCHOOLS

AREAS OF ACTION

PURPOSE		PEOPLE	
It's About the Mission, Not the Mission Statement	High Expectations for Each and Every Student	Building Communities of Learners	Teachers Are the Silver Bullet

PROCESS

CREATING A COHERENT SYSTEM
FOR CONTINUOUS IMPROVEMENT

High-impact leaders ask themselves every day, "How am I leading purpose? How am I supporting people? How am I ensuring that school processes support the work and effort to become a high-impact school?"

References

Barth, R. (2001). *Learning by heart*. San Francisco: Jossey-Bass.

Beck, L., & Murphy, J. (1993). *Understanding the principalship: Metaphorical themes 1920s–1990s*. New York: Teachers College Press.

Boaler, J. (2006, February). Promoting respectful learning. *Educational Leadership, 63*(5), 74–78.

Cross, C., & Rice, R. (2000). The role of the principal as instructional leader in a standards-driven system. *National Association of Secondary School Principals Bulletin, 84*(620), 61–65.

Donaldson, G. (2001). *Cultivating leadership in schools: Connecting people, purpose and practice*. New York: Teachers College Press.

Dougherty, C. (2006). *Identifying and studying high-performing schools* (NCEA Issue Brief #1). Austin, TX: National Center for Educational Accountability.

Dufour, R. (2002). The learning-centered principal. *Educational Leadership, 59*(8), 12–15.

Dyer, M. (2000). *What is takes—10 capacities for initiating and sustaining school improvement at the elementary level*. Providence, RI: Northeast and Islands Regional Educational Laboratory.

Elmore, R. (2000). *Building a new structure for school leadership*. Washington, DC: The Albert Shanker Institute.

Fenwick, L., & Collins-Pierce, M. (2001, March). The principal shortage: Crisis or opportunity. *Principal, 10*(43), 25–32.

Flanary, R. A. (2005, October). *Breakthrough schools: What works in high school reform*. Retrieved June 9, 2007, from http://www.reinventingeducation.org/RE3Web/newsletters/20051001/article02.htm

Fullan, M. (2003). *The moral imperative of school leadership*. Thousand Oaks, CA: Corwin Press.

Hale, E., & Rollins, K. (2006, June). Leading the way to increased student learning. *Principal Leadership, 6*(10), 6–9.

Heck, R., & Marcoulides, G. (1993, May). Principal leadership behaviors and school achievement. *National Association of Secondary School Principals Bulletin, 77*(553), 20–28.

Johnson, J., & Asera, R. (1999). *Hope for urban education: A study of nine-high-performing high-poverty urban elementary schools.* Retrieved June 18, 2007, from www.ed.gov/pubs/urbanhope/index.html

Kannapel, P., & Clements, S. (2005). *Inside the black box of high-performing high-poverty schools.* Retrieved June 7, 2007, from http://www.prichardcommittee.org/Ford%20Study/FordReportJE.pdf

Knapp, M. (1993). *Academic challenge for children of poverty.* Retrieved June 7, 2007, from www.eric.ed.gov:80/ERICWebPortal/custom/portlets/recordDetails/detailmini.jsp?_nfpb=true&_&ERICExtSearch_SearchValue_0=ED358213&ERICExtSearch_SearchType_0=eric_accno&accno=ED358213

Lemahieu, P., Roy, P., & Foss, H. (1997, January). Through a lens clearly: A model to guide the instructional leadership of principals. *Urban Education, 31*(5), 582–608.

Lewis, A., & Paik, S. (2001). *Add it up: Using research to improve education for low-income and minority students.* Retrieved June 17, 2007, from www.prrac.org/pubs_aiu.pdf

Marriott, D. (2001, September). Managing school culture. *Principal 81*(1), 75–77.

McTighe, J., & O'Connor, K. (2005, November). Seven practices for effective learning. *Educational Leadership, 63*(30), 10–17.

National Staff Development Council. (2001). *Collaboration skills.* Retrieved July 26, 2007, from http://www.nsdc.org/standards/collaborationskills.cfm

Quick, D., & Quick, C. (2000). *High poverty—High success: Schools that defy the odds.* Portland, OR: Northwest Regional Educational Laboratory.

Reeves, D. (2007, March). Closing the implementation gap. *Educational Leadership, 64*(6), 85–86.

Robison, S., Stempel, A., & McCree, I. (2005). *Gaining traction, gaining ground: How some high schools accelerate learning for struggling students.* Washington, DC: Education Trust.

Saphier, J., & D'Auria, J. (1993). *How to bring vision to school improvement: Through core outcomes, commitments and beliefs.* Carlisle, MA: Research for Better Teaching.

Schmoker, M. (1999). *Results: The key to continuous school improvement* (2nd ed.). Alexandria, VA: Association of Supervision and Curriculum Development.

Shannon, S. (2003). *Nine characteristics of high-performing schools.* Retrieved June 10, 2007, from www.k12.wa.us/research/pubdocs/pdf/9charactfor%20SIP.pdf

Smith, L. (2001). Can schools really change? *Education Week, 20*(21), 30–33.

Southern Regional Education Board. (2004). *2004 outstanding practices using rigor, relevance, and relationships to improve student achievement: How some schools do it.* Retrieved July 29, 2007, from http://www.sreb.org/programs/hstw/Outstanding/op2004.asp

Steel, C., & Craig, E. (2006, May). Reworking industrial models, exploring contemporary ideas, and fostering teacher leadership. *Phi Delta Kappan, 87*(9), 676–680.

Tirozzi, G. N. (2001, February). The artistry of leadership: The evolving role of the secondary school principal. *Phi Delta Kappan, 82*(6), 434–439.

Villegas, A., & Lucas, T. (2007, March). The culturally responsive teacher. *Educational Leadership, 64*(6), 28–33.

Williams, T., Perry, M., Oregón, I., Brazil, N., Hakuta, K., Haertel, E., et al. (2007). *Similar English learner students, different results: Why do some schools do better? A follow-up analysis, based on a large-scale survey of California elementary schools serving low-income and EL students.* Mountain View, CA: Edsource.